ISBN 979-8-8581138-2-9

Halima Publishing ltd
Henley-on-Thames, Oxfordshire U.K.
www.halimapublishing.co.uk

By Yasmin Watson
Illustrations by Hana Horack-Elyafi

SECOND EDITION

A Young Person's Guide to

Science

in the

Qur'an

"And We made from water every living thing"

Science in the Qur'an

Discovering Scientific Secrets in the Holy Qur'an

CONTENTS

1. Introduction

The Qur'an is a holy book that was revealed to the Prophet Muhammad ﷺ almost 1500 years ago. Over the centuries, Islamic scholars have studied and interpreted the holy text and have recently discovered that there are verses that seem to relate to modern scientific discoveries, things that we only understand now in the 20th and 21st centuries. There are specific verses that relate to topics such as the nature of the Universe, genetics, atomic structure, the speed of light, plate tectonics, and many more. In this book, we compare these verses from the Qur'an in the light of modern science.

Before we begin to explore these subjects, we ask a few questions about the Islamic view of science and provide a brief history of science in Islam.

Science Versus Religion?

People often think of religion and science as completely different subjects, and at opposite ends of the way we understand the Universe we live in. This conflict began in Europe in the 16th century with discoveries by scientists such as Nicolaus Copernicus, Galileo Galilei, Sir Isaac Newton and Charles Darwin and continues to this present day. These scientists wanted to observe the natural world to understand how things worked and some of these new findings did not match up to Christian religious thought at that time.

Although Darwin and scientists from that era all believed in God, scientists who followed them started to remove God from the equation as they made more and more discoveries and wanted an empirical, fact-based method of evidence to form logical conclusions. Nowadays, there are some scientists who believe in God and some do not.

What is an Islamic view about science?

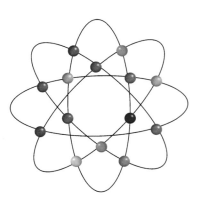

Where do Muslims stand in the argument? Muslims believe that God is the Creator of everything, but also that we have been given an intellect to understand the world around us. Islam itself is based on proof and reason with Muslims as early as the 9th century embracing the sciences, which resulted in many great advances, notably the beginnings of modern surgery, astrophysics and algebra. For many Muslims, evidence in the natural world leads to greater knowledge and understanding of God's creation. Dinosaurs, trilobites and ancient algae are not a threat to Islamic belief, rather, it is a confirmation of the power of Allah. Any new evidence in the sciences only serves to provide more signs of the Greatness of Allah. Muslims believe that Allah can choose to unfold creation as He likes, He sets up the laws and the functioning of the Universe with the Divine power that the Qur'an refers to:

"His Command is only when He intends a thing that He says, 'Be' and it is."
(Ya Siin 36:82)

Brief Overview of the History of Science in Islam

The sciences are a very important part of Islamic history. From as early as the 9th century A.D., there has been a fascination about the world we live in, with amazing inventions and world leading scientific discoveries.

Medicine

The work of doctors and surgeons such as Al Kindi (801-873), Al-Zahrawi (936-1013), Ibn Sina, (980-1037) and Ibn Al Nafis (1213-1288) all formed the basis of modern surgery and medicine and they were far more advanced than Western medical practices at the time.

Astronomy

As early as the 9th century, Muslims began a scientific study of the stars and the planets. Huge observatories were built in places like Baghdad and Damascus.

Algebra

Abu Abdallah Muhammad ibn Musa al-Khwarizmi (d.850) was a Persian mathematician who developed some of the fundamentals of algebra that are still used today. He worked at the 'House of Wisdom' in Baghdad in the 9th century.

Modern Day Scientists

Muslims around the world continue to work in the field of science, winning the Nobel Prize such as Mohammad Abdul Salam, who won the Nobel Prize in 1979 for his work in particle physics as well as Ahmad Zewail in 1999 for Chemistry and Aziz Sancar in 2015 for his work on DNA repair.

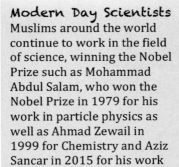

About this book

In this book we highlight the ancient Qur'anic verses that have been identified as having links with modern science and compare them side-by-side to many scientific facts and discoveries to find the remarkable links and comparisons. As we explore the different chapters on astrophysics, geology, chemistry, particle physics and more, we can wonder at the immense complexity, enormity and minute detail found in our magnificent Universe. The Qur'an itself has many secrets to uncover and we may begin to understand what the Prophet Muhammad ﷺ meant when he said about Qur'an: *"Its wonders never cease."(i)*

Activity Notes

In each chapter find ideas for experiments and research at home. Ideal for all young scientists!

8

1. The Holy Quran & Secret Codes

"Alif, Laam, Miim."
(Surat Al-Baqara 2:1)

تَنْزِيلُ الْكِتَبِ مِنَ اللهِ الْعَزِيزِ الْحَكِيمِ
إِنَّ فِي السَّمَوَتِ وَالْأَرْضِ لَأَيَتٍ لِّلْمُؤْمِنِينَ

"Haa, Miim. The revelation of the book is from Allah. Verily in
the Heavens and the Earth are signs for those who believe."
(Surat Al-Jathiya 45:1-3)

The Holy Qur'an
- What is the Qur'an?

"Verily, in the Heavens and the Earth are signs for those who believe." (Al-Jathiya:3)

Muslims believe the Holy Qur'an was revealed to humanity through the Holy Prophet Muhammad ﷺ via the Archangel Gabriel عليه السلام

The Qur'an is said to not be of creation but from the Essence of Allah Himself ﷻ

The Qur'an is essentially about the soul's journey to Allah through stories, parables, revelations and guidance.

It is precise in its format, its Arabic language beautiful and elegantly rhythmic. The Qur'an is known to be a source of enlightenment and said to contain the knowledge of everything, which on the surface may not be obvious, but is increasingly apparent according to the level of faith a reader has.

The Qur'an is very easy to remember, so much so that millions of people are 'Hafiz' Qur'an, having memorised the entire Qur'an by heart.

Another miracle is that the Qur'an has never altered since the time of its revelation.

This decorated page shows the love and care the artist spent trying to express the greatness of the Qur'an. Muslims believe that there is nothing comparable on Earth.

Secret Codes in Qur'an

"Alif, Lam, Meem."

Al- Baqara:2

There are plenty of mysteries and codes to unlock within the Holy Qur'an. The Qur'an encourages people to contemplate and meditate on the ancient verses, to discover the mysteries and the hidden codes contained within. If everything were obvious, there would be no pursuit of knowledge. Both religion and science are interested in uncovering the mysteries of life. Many of today's scientific mysteries are also like secret codes waiting to be uncovered.

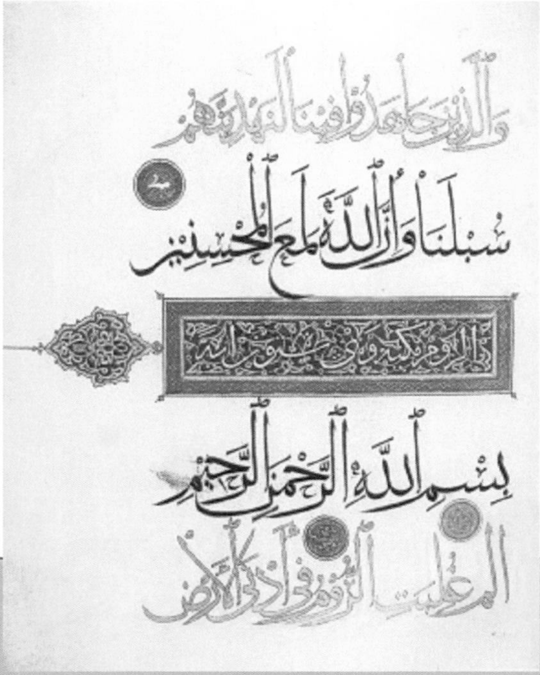

The study of the Qur'an always requires learning from a teacher. We cannot think we can just read through and understand it all, as verses can be misinterpreted. Those practised in the meaning of the Qur'an spend their whole lives improving their levels of understanding. There are many fine *tafsirs* or commentaries of the Qur'an by respected scholars who explore the meanings of each verse, with thousands of books written on the subject.

Mysteriously, some letters appear on their own at the beginning of some chapters in the Qur'an. The Scholars will say that each letter in the Arabic alphabet is said to have a meaning.

For example, the second chapter, Al-Baqara, begins with Alif, Lam, Mim, three Arabic letters. According to Tanwir al-Miqbas min Tafsir Ibn Abbas, who was a Companion of the Prophet Muhammad ﷺ, these letters may represent Alif for Allah, Lam for the Archangel Gabriel and Mim for Muhammad ﷺ.

In Arabic writing, the letter Alif cannot be joined with any other letter. This represents Allah asking people to not join any partners with Him.

The letter Alif always points upwards as seen in this beautiful Arabic calligraphy.

In Islamic Sacred Sciences, numbers are very important and provide symbolic meanings. If we think of how computer programmes are made, using just 1 and 0, similarly it is said that the knowledge of Creation can be contained in numerical symbols. It is interesting to think in a symbolic way so that new meanings may become apparent when we look at numbers, especially in the Qur'an. Also, in the science of dream interpretations, numbers appearing in the dream may represent different things.

1 – The Creator, the Absolute Unity of Allah.

2 –Represents the unfolding of Creation or the Prophet Muhammad ﷺ. The number 2 may also represent parents, or marriage or a birth of a child.

3 – A significant number in numerology. Many verses of Quran are recited three times.

4 - Four seasons, four elements.

5 – The 5 senses, the 5 daily prayers.

6 – Represents balance, externally and internally or the days of Creation.

7 – Perfection of the soul, the seven Heavens or days of the week.

8 – Eternal life.

9 – Complete surrender. Also could symbolise a person's life, birth (being pregnant for 9 months) and 9 being the last number, represents death.

10 – Represents perfection of one's religion. 10 also reverts to 1, because two digits can be added together to find a single number.

12

3. Numbers

بِسْمِ ٱللَّهِ ٱلرَّحْمَٰنِ ٱلرَّحِيمِ

ٱلشَّمْسُ وَٱلْقَمَرُ بِحُسْبَانٍ ۝

"The sun and moon (move) by precise calculation."
(The All Merciful 55:5)

وَبَنَيْنَا فَوْقَكُمْ سَبْعًا شِدَادًا ۝

"We have built above you seven mighty Heavens."

(The Event 78:12)

Numbers

We have already seen how important numbers are in the Holy Qur'an. In science, numbers are also very important. Numbers may remind you of sums at school and banks and money. Scientists however know that everything in the Universe can be described in numbers. That is why scientists can work out amazing things about the Universe, work out how to build machines and write computer programs using numbers. Without numbers we would not have been able to build any of the modern things that we are used to such as cars, tall buildings, space shuttles or medical equipment.

The verse of Qur'an above says that the Sun and the Moon follow movements that have been precisely calculated. Indeed, Scientists believe that if the characteristics of the Sun and the Moon were different, life may not have emerged on Earth. The Sun provides essential warmth and light as well as being the gravitational centre of the Solar System, holding the planets in their orbits, all of which have an effect on the system as a whole. The Moon has the effect of slowing the Earth's spin to the speed suitable for life to emerge as well as affecting the tides and movement of all water. Another intriguing fact is that the relative size and distance both of the Moon and the Sun to Earth means that both objects appear the same size in the sky although are actually vastly different in size.

Science also tells us that everything is precisely calculated in the Universe, for instance:

1. If, at the time of the Big Bang, the force was 1/millionth more or less powerful the Universe would not have come into existence.

2. If the strong nuclear force was decreased by just 2%, the structure of the atom would not hold itself together and hydrogen would be the only element in the Universe.

3. If the gravitational force was reduced even a fraction, stars would not ignite and galaxies would not be formed.

If any of these changed even a tiny bit, the whole Universe would not exist.

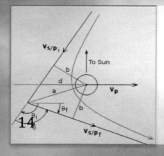

Astrophysicist and engineers will spend many years working out and building space vehicles in order to launch one ship out of Earth's gravity and to its destination in space. Extremely complex calculations are made in order to do this, ensuring the success of the mission and safety of the crew.

Here on Earth, everything can be looked at in terms of numbers. We see some very obvious signs in nature and they are some of the most beautiful natural forms on Earth. These basic fundamentals of design are used in engineering, construction and mathematics.

Fractals

"Mathematics is the language with which God has written the Universe." Galileo Galilei

Fractals can also be seen in nature. They are interesting because they are actually extremely simple, yet the constant repetition forms spirals, branches and patterns. Imagine how a tree or shell grows or the cellular neural patterns in our brains, these all have a fractal-like growth pattern. Fractals can also be created by geometry and algebra. In algebra, you can input simple formula to a computer and produce amazing images that continue forever.

Binary Code

Did you know that computer programs create whole realities using binary system which is ultimately just a series of 0's and 1's?

"Your computer successfully creates the illusion that it contains photographs, letters, songs, and movies. All it really contains is bits (kind of a switch), lots of them, patterned in ways you can't see." (Hal Abelson, Ken Ledeen, Harry Lewis, in "Blown to Bits"

The programmes then condense the information into geometrically balanced patterns and these patterns form various computer languages.

Activity Notes:

Explore your garden or a park – what shapes and geometry can you see? Make a scrapbook with drawings and objects of things you have noticed.

Amazing Number Facts

In the Holy Qur'an, all the verses and layout are precisely ordered. The verses were ordered according to the instructions of the Holy Prophet ﷺ. The structure of the Qur'an is so complicated, yet so balanced that it is impossible to reproduce it. Here are some profound number facts found in the Qur'an:

Land and Sea

Scientists have calculated that 71% of the Earth is covered in Oceans and Seas and 29% is land.

Amazingly, if you count the number of times 'land' and 'sea' appears in the Qur'an, this works out proportionally almost exactly the same.

The word count of 'land' is 13 times and 32 times for Sea, giving a total of 45. If you work this out proportionally, the result is 28.9% for land and 71.1% for sea.

6 Days of Creation

"Indeed, your Lord is Allah , who created the Heavens and the Earth in six days..." (7:54)

The Holy Qur'an has specified the number of days of Creation as 6. There are 6,666 verses in the Qur'an. If you add those digits, we have 24, if we add 2+4 we have 6 again. There are also 114 verses in Qur'an, again this equals 6.

in the Holy Qur'an

19 – The Hidden Code

- "Bismillahirahmanirahim"(In the name of Allah, the Beneficent, the Merciful) has 19 Arabic letters.
- The number of times the word "Allah" appears adds up to a multiple of 19.
- The sum of all digits mentioned in the Qur'an adds up to a multiple of 19.
- The sum of all verse numbers that the word 'Allah' appears adds up to a multiple of 19.
- The sum of chapters' numbers adds up to a multiple of 19.
- The number of chapters (Suras) in the Qur'an adds up to a multiple of 19.
- If you add the letters of Muhammad ☉, Ali (r), Fatima (r), Hassan (r) and Hussain (r), they come to 19.
- Some chapters start with letters that have no obvious meaning. When we add the number of occurrences of those letters in their chapters we always get a multiple of 19.
- If you add 1+9 it makes 10 which added together makes 1, representing Allah.

If anyone changed a single word containing those letters in the Quran, the signature would have been broken.

Men and Women Populations

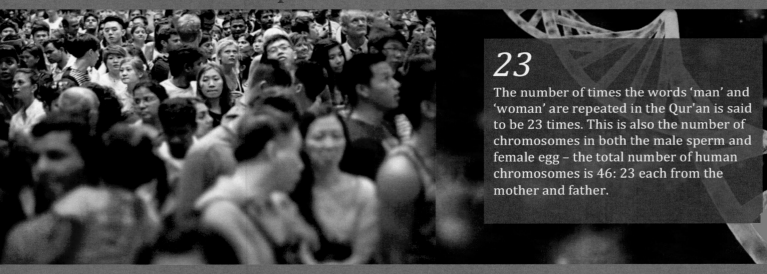

23

The number of times the words 'man' and 'woman' are repeated in the Qur'an is said to be 23 times. This is also the number of chromosomes in both the male sperm and female egg – the total number of human chromosomes is 46: 23 each from the mother and father.

Days, Months and Years

In the Qur'an, it is reported that 'day' is repeated 365 times in singular form, while its plural and dual forms 'days' together are repeated 30 times. The number of repetitions of the word 'month' is 12.

Activity notes:

Investigate these number coincidences - perhaps adding up the number of chapters and looking at the significance of numbers in Islam. You can also add up the numerical value of the letters in your name to get a personalised meaning.

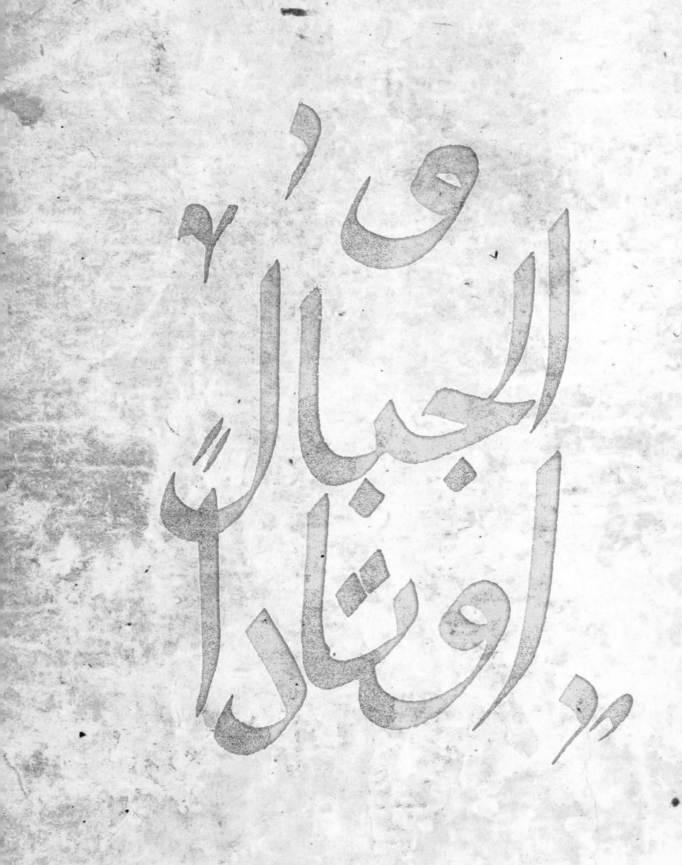

4. Mountains

وَٱلْأَرْضَ مَدَدْنَٰهَا وَأَلْقَيْنَا فِيهَا رَوَٰسِىَ وَأَنۢبَتْنَا فِيهَا مِن كُلِّ زَوْجٍۭ بَهِيجٍ ۝

"And the Earth We have spread it out and set therein anchoring mountains to balance it as it spins. And it is We alone who caused to grow in it every kind of beautiful growth." (Surat Qaf 50:7)

أَلَمْ نَجْعَلِ ٱلْأَرْضَ مِهَٰدًا ۝

وَٱلْجِبَالَ أَوْتَادًا ۝

"Have We not make the Earth a resting place?
And the mountains as stakes?" (Surat an-Naba 78:6-7)

وَتَرَى ٱلْجِبَالَ تَحْسَبُهَا جَامِدَةً وَهِىَ تَمُرُّ مَرَّ ٱلسَّحَابِ صُنْعَ ٱللَّهِ ٱلَّذِىٓ أَتْقَنَ كُلَّ شَىْءٍ إِنَّهُۥ خَبِيرٌۢ بِمَا تَفْعَلُونَ ۝

"You see the mountains and think them firmly fixed: but they shall pass away as the clouds pass away: (such is) the artistry of Allah, Who disposes of all things in perfect order: for He is well acquainted with all that you do."
(Surat I-Naml 27:88)

Mountains

You see the mountains and think they are firmly fixed: but they will pass (as the) passing (of) the clouds. (Such is) the artistry of Allah, Who disposes of all things in perfect order: for He knows all what you do. (The Ants:88)

Mountains are the most impressive aspect of the surface of the Earth. Thousands of metres high, they inspire awe and seem unmovable. In this verse, the Qur'an mentions that in fact, they are not as permanent as they seem. In the 20th Century, Geographers discovered that indeed the Earth's crust is moving and the mountains along with it! Perhaps the verse is also reminding people that nothing in this world is permanent, even the mountains will pass like the clouds.

Scientists speculate that at the time of the early dinosaurs the Earth looked very different, with one main land mass called Pangea.

The Piqiang Fault, a northwest trending fault in the Taklamakan Desert south of the Tien Shan Mountains, China

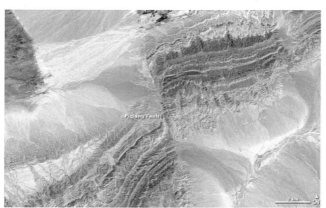

If we look at the history of the Earth over millions of years we can see the huge changes that have taken place. This is referred to as Continental Drift - the Earth's crust slowly but surely drifting into new formations. Over millions of years the continents have drifted to the places we know now.

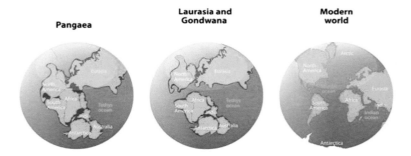

This is because the Earth's crust is a comparatively thin layer, with the next layer more fluid. The forces within the huge mass of Earth put pressure on the crust and gradually push the tectonic plates either away from each other or towards each other. As two plates move together, they rise up to form mountains, and when they move apart they form fissures and earthquakes. These zones are called fault lines and are where we find volcanoes, earthquakes and geysers. These fault lines can be from a few kilometres to thousands of kilometres like the San Andreas Fault in California.

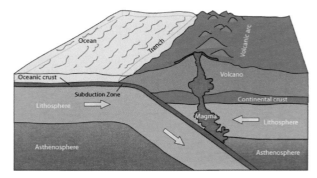

"Have We not make the Earth a resting place? And the mountains as stakes?" [An-Naba:6-7]

In the verse above, the Qur'an indicates that mountains have roots by using the word 'stakes' to describe them. In fact, mountains do have deep roots. They may assist in slowing down the tectonic movement of the crust as is referred to in the verse; *"And the Earth, We have spread it out and set therein anchoring mountains, to balance it as it spins."* (al Qaf-7)

Geologist predict that Mount Everest, the height of which is approximately 9 km above ground, has a corresponding root, possibly as deep as 60 km, to stabilize the immense weight. We can imagine how this is formed with the movement of the tectonic plates crushing the two pieces of land together.

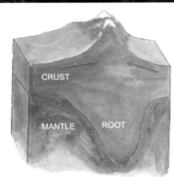

"And the earth, We have spread it out and set therein anchoring mountains, to balance it as it spins." (al Qaf-7)

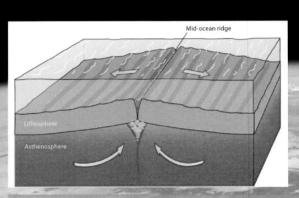

New land (or crust) is created at the divergent boundaries. These fissures are also a way for the Earth to release pressures generated deep below the surface. Again the Qur'an describes 'spreading out the Earth', which is a good description for the tectonic movements that shape our landscape. Without the tectonic movements, the land would be very flat, lacking in features.

The Red Sea is an example of a divergent boundary. We can see from this satellite picture that it looks as if it is being torn apart. The land is still moving and the Red Sea is getting wider every year.

Activity notes:
Find a small dish and some plasticine. Mould your own island with geographical features such as mountains, volcanoes, lakes and rivers. Push the plasticine together to form taller mountains. You can add water to your landscape as well, filling up the lakes and seas.

21

وَأَنْزَلْنَا الْحَدِيدَ فِيهِ بَأْسٌ شَدِيدٌ

5. Iron

بِسْمِ اللهِ الرَّحْمٰنِ الرَّحِيْمِ

لَقَدْ اَرْسَلْنَا رُسُلَنَا بِالْبَيِّنٰتِ وَ اَنْزَلْنَا مَعَهُمُ الْكِتٰبَ وَ الْمِيْزَانَ لِيَقُوْمَ النَّاسُ بِالْقِسْطِ ۚ وَ اَنْزَلْنَا الْحَدِيْدَ فِيْهِ بَأْسٌ شَدِيْدٌ وَّ مَنَافِعُ لِلنَّاسِ وَ لِيَعْلَمَ اللهُ مَنْ يَّنْصُرُهُ وَ رُسُلَهُ بِالْغَيْبِ ۚ اِنَّ اللهَ قَوِيٌّ عَزِيْزٌ ۩

"Very truly, We have sent down Messengers to humanity with clear and miraculous proofs that confirm their messages.
And We sent down with each of them a Heavenly Book to guide their people, along with the just balance, so that people might establish justice in the Earth.

Moreover, We sent down iron from the Heavens, in which there is a mighty force, and in which there are many benefits for all people; and so that Allah might make known who supports Him and His Messengers, though unseen.
Indeed, Allah alone is all-powerful, overpowering."
(Al-Hadid 57:25)

"And We sent down Iron, wherein is a mighty power, as well as many benefits for mankind." Iron 57:25

Iron is a common element that we find on Earth and forms 32.1% of the mass of Earth. Where did iron come from? Most people think that iron originally comes from the Earth.

Amazingly, scientists have discovered that iron is found all over the Universe and is actually created in the extreme temperatures of massive stars. They have discovered that iron cannot be made on Earth and is in fact sent from the stars..."*And we sent down iron*"(57:25). As stars evolve, the process known as nucleosynthesis creates heavier and heavier elements. If the star is massive enough, nucleosynthesis will result in an iron core. When the star reaches the end of its life cycle, it explodes in a supernova distributing everything in the Universe.

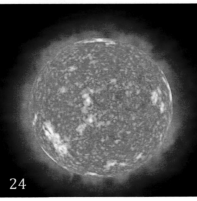

Scientists believe that the Earth was formed by heavy atoms such as iron, clumping together, revolving and gradually forming our planet. Some of the original heat that was present when the Earth was created still exists today, it is thought, in the Earth's molten core. This core is extremely hot and is in fact, it is almost the same temperature as the surface of the sun – 5700 degrees Kelvin.

The iron at the core is kept at this temperature due to the immense pressure of the gravity of Earth. The core pressure of the Earth is 330-360 Gpa which is 3 million times greater than the Earth's atmosphere pressure on the surface. Scientists can only guess at the exact circumstances in the Earth's core because it would actually be easier to get to the surface of Pluto.

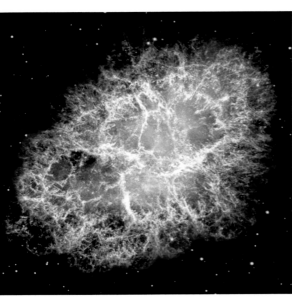

The Crab Nebulae after a supernova explosion, sending out millions of different particles, including heavy elements such as iron and other metals to enrich the galaxy with more materials.

IRON FACTS
Symbol: Fe
Stable isotopes of iron:
^{54}Fe, ^{56}Fe, ^{57}Fe, ^{58}Fe
Number of protons: 26
Number of electrons: 26
Melting point: 1811 K
Boiling point: 3134 K

The Holy Qur'an predicts the atomic weight and the number of neutrons in iron.

Do the numbers 57 and 26 mean anything to you when you think of iron? Someone who knows their Periodic Table, will know that iron 57 is one of the isotopes or variations of iron. The chapter 'Iron' is the 57th chapter in the Qur'an.

Iron is also the 26th element in the periodic table, which means it has 26 electrons and 26 protons. If we look at where the word 'iron' first appears in this chapter of Qur'an, it is in verse 25 but if we count the 'Bismillahirahmanirahim' as the first verse, we can count this as verse 26 - its place in the periodic table and if we count the 'Bismillah' again, there are in total 30 verses in the sura - the amount of neutrons in one of the isotopes of iron.

The Holy Prophet ﷺ asked his Companions to place 'Iron' as the 57th sura, long before the Periodic Table was compiled and the verses appear in the exact same order from when it was originally revealed.

The crystal structure of iron

Scientists have found out that iron is the strongest element in the Universe. Until the discovery of pulsar stars, scientists thought that no atoms could survive the huge pressure of stellar collapse. But now we know that pulsars have rotating iron cores. This means iron has one of the strongest bound nucleus of all the elements and certainly contains a 'mighty power'.

Numeric values of the word
Al Hadid
*Alif-1, Lam-30, ha – 8, dal- 4, yaa-10, dal – 4 = **57***

"....as well as many benefits for mankind."

We use iron for all sorts of things from tools to cooking to gates...little did the Iron Age Man know that the iron he was mining came from the stars! We have found objects made of iron dating from 3500 BC.

Records show that iron was smelted in China in the 16th Century to produce pig iron and wrought iron as this illustration shows.

Iron can also be refined into steel and even stronger metal, used for almost all building.

Homework notes:
Iron filings experiment:
Buy some iron filings and a magnet.
Place a piece of paper over the magnet and carefully sprinkle the iron on top. A very interesting pattern will emerge.

وَجَعَلْنَا مِنَ الْمَاءِ كُلَّ شَيْءٍ حَيٍّ

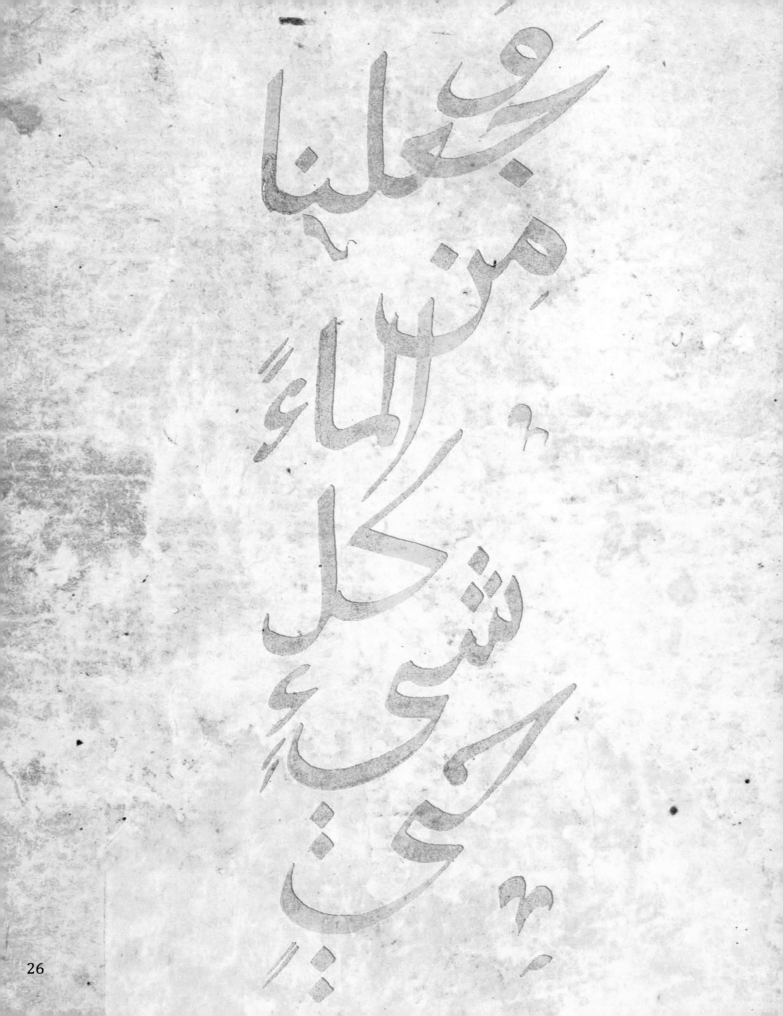

6. Life made from Water

بِسْمِ اللهِ الرَّحْمٰنِ الرَّحِيْمِ

اَوَلَمْ يَرَ الَّذِيْنَ كَفَرُوْا اَنَّ السَّمٰوٰتِ وَ الْاَرْضَ كَانَتَا رَتْقًا فَفَتَقْنٰهُمَا ۗ وَجَعَلْنَا مِنَ الْمَآءِ كُلَّ شَيْءٍ حَيٍّ ۗ اَفَلَا يُؤْمِنُوْنَ ۞

"Have those who disbelieve not seen by the knowledge they acquire that the Heavens and the Earth were conjoined as one mass, then We separated them – and that We made every living thing therein from water? Will they not, then, believe in Allah's Oneness?" (The Prophets 21:30)

وَ اللهُ خَلَقَ كُلَّ دَآبَّةٍ مِّنْ مَّآءٍ ۚ فَمِنْهُمْ مَّنْ يَّمْشِيْ عَلٰى بَطْنِهٖ ۚ وَ مِنْهُمْ مَّنْ يَّمْشِيْ عَلٰى رِجْلَيْنِ ۚ وَ مِنْهُمْ مَّنْ يَّمْشِيْ عَلٰى اَرْبَعٍ ۚ يَخْلُقُ اللهُ مَا يَشَآءُ ۗ اِنَّ اللهَ عَلٰى كُلِّ شَيْءٍ قَدِيْرٌ ۞

"Moreover, Allah created every living creature from water. Yet of them are those that go on their bellies. And of them are those that walk on two legs. And of them are those that walk on four.
Allah creates whatever He so wills. Indeed Allah is powerful over all things." (The Light 24:45)

هَلْ اَتٰى عَلَى الْاِنْسَانِ حِيْنٌ مِّنَ الدَّهْرِ لَمْ يَكُنْ شَيْئًا مَّذْكُوْرًا ۞

"Has there not been over Man a long period of time before Humans were even mentioned?" (Mankind 76:1)

Life Made From Water

This Holy verse indicates that life comes from water. If we look at the current scientific evidence about life from water, we find that this is true in many different ways, individually, and in life on Earth as a whole. We can also wonder at the metaphorical meanings, as every verse from the Qur'an has many levels of understanding, perhaps oceans of meanings.

Water in chemistry

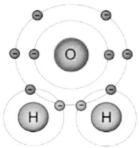

What is water from a chemical point of view? Water is made from two elements, hydrogen and oxygen, H2O. With the perfect balance of two hydrogen and one oxygen atom, pure water is made. Water is unique as it can change states from solid, liquid to gas depending on temperature.

There are two hydrogen atoms for every one atom of oxygen. Even though hydrogen can be very explosive, when bonded with another hydrogen and an oxygen atom, water is produced. We find hydrogen in 75% of all visible mass and is the main building block of the Universe, being found in stars, organic life and water. This is because hydrogen bonds very easily with other atoms, being very simple in its structure. Scientists think that hydrogen was one of the three original elements that were produced by the Big Bang along with helium and traces of lithium.

Oxygen is the third most common element in the Universe. It began to accumulate on the Earth 2.5 billion years ago and is essential to all life. We find oxygen in about 20% of our atmosphere and about 50% of the Earths crust and is produced by the constant action of photosynthesis.

HYDROGEN
Symbol: H2
Atomic weight :1.00794
About: 75% of all visible mass of the Universe. Found in all life and stars.
1st element in the periodic table

OXYGEN
Symbol: O
Atomic weight: 15.99
About: Readily forms compounds
Third most common element
Found in all organic life
Number 8 in periodic table

Did Life on Earth First Appear in the Seas and Oceans?

Scientists believe that living creatures *originated in the sea*. The earliest fossil records show that the earliest life forms were all living in the seas and oceans, initially single cell bacteria, then millions of years later creatures emerged like this trilobite from the Cambrian period and Ammonites in the Devonian period. The Tiktaalik Roseae, pictured opposite, is a fish type creature that possibly emerged from the oceans 375 million years ago.

"Has there not been over Man a long period of time before Humans were even mentioned?" (Mankind:1)

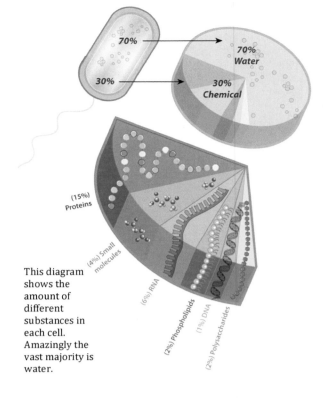

70%

70% Water

30%

30% Chemical

(15%) Proteins

(4%) Small molecules

(6%) RNA

(2%) Phospholipids

(1%) DNA

(2%) Polysaccharides

This diagram shows the amount of different substances in each cell. Amazingly the vast majority is water.

"Allah created every animal from water."
(Light:45)

All living cells are made with 70% water. That means all living creatures on the Earth are mostly made of water. If you cut yourself however, you do not see floods of water coming out, but we do see blood. If we look under a microscope, at the blood cells, there is a lot of water contained within the plasma fluid. Its almost like there is billions of tiny packages of water in each of our bodies.

Life beginning with water

Each human, animal, insect, bird, & reptile, in fact all life on Earth, begins that life with water. Life begins in eggs or inside mammals in an environment full of liquid. Trees and plants also need water to germinate the seeds. Have a look at the different examples.

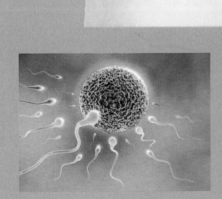

Human life begins with two tiny cells, these unite and then a new baby grows within the mothers' womb, surrounded by a special fluid called amniotic fluid. This also protects the baby from bumps.

Activity notes:

From the pictures to the left, can you match which egg or seed goes with which each living thing?

29

مَرَجَ الْبَحْرَيْنِ يَلْتَقِيَانِ

7. Two Seas Meet But Do Not Mix

بِسْمِ اللهِ الرَّحْمٰنِ الرَّحِيْمِ

مَرَجَ الْبَحْرَيْنِ يَلْتَقِيٰنِ ۝

بَيْنَهُمَا بَرْزَخٌ لَّا يَبْغِيٰنِ ۝

"He released the two seas, meeting (side by side); between them is a barrier that neither of them transgress." (The All-Merciful 55:19-20)

وَهُوَ الَّذِيْ مَرَجَ الْبَحْرَيْنِ هٰذَا عَذْبٌ فُرَاتٌ وَّهٰذَا مِلْحٌ أُجَاجٌ ۚ وَ

جَعَلَ بَيْنَهُمَا بَرْزَخًا وَّحِجْرًا مَّحْجُوْرًا ۝

"And He is the One Who has merged together the flow of the two great waters: Who let the two seas flow; One palpable and sweet and the other salty and bitter. Yet He has made a seamless divide, a barrier that bars their intermingling." (al-Furqan 25:53)

Two Seas Meet But Do Not Mix

"He released the two seas, meeting (side by side); Between them is a barrier that neither of them transgress."
(Ar-Rahman, 55:19-20)

The Qur'an describes how there are seas that meet but do not blend or mix together. Oceanographers have discovered that there are at least three cases like this on Earth where one ocean meets another but the two waters do not mix and each ocean or sea has its own fish, temperature and salinity.

The Gulf of Alaska, Cape Agulhas in South Africa and the Strait of Gibraltar, where the Atlantic Ocean meets the Mediterranean Sea, are good examples of this. It is amazing that the ancient text refers to this surprising feature of the Oceans and Seas.

A lion fish, two rock fish and a starfish from the Atlantic ocean

The Gulf of Alaska

The picture shows two different ocean water bodies meeting in the middle of the Alaskan Gulf. This happens when glaciers of fresh water melt and then flow to join the other ocean water that is saltier. Because of the difference in the salinity and densities of these two meeting ocean water bodies, a surface tension develops between them that acts like a thin wall and does not allow them to mix.

The Qur'an may be speaking of something much greater than this occurrence but these physical wonders appear perhaps as a sign. We can wonder again about the knowledge from a time and place far removed from modern scientific discoveries.

In some cases where two oceans or seas meet, there are rough waters and terrible storms.
Cape Agulhas, for instance, is perilous for many ships, especially in the days of the Clipper routes, because of fierce storms and enormous waves as high as 100 feet.
Cape Horn, at the southern-most tip of South America is also famous for extremely dangerous waters.

In the verse above the Qur'an describes two seas, or bodies of water, one salty and the other sweet. River wildlife for example, is very different from that of the oceans. Each environment has its own unique wildlife, for example, there is a lot of difference between fresh water fish and salt-water fish. River fish would die if put in the ocean and the other way around. The Qur'an may also be referring to the difference between sweet drinking water and bitter salty water that can be compared to the difference between the beauty of Paradise and the difficulties of the world.

Marine Biologists have found that when a fish comes near a different type of water, the fish comes to the edge of the ocean, river or sea, they then descend and go back, not crossing into the other area. Quarantine areas have also been discovered in some areas, between the two waters. The fish spends some time adjusting and then can pass to the other ocean.

There are no Mediterranean holidays for this Atlantic fish!

Case Study: Cape Algulhas

Cape Algulhas, on the south most tip of Africa, has completely different temperatures and aquatic life depending if you are on the Indian Ocean side or the Atlantic side! We can compare the two coastal towns of Durban and Port Nolloth, both on the same latitude.

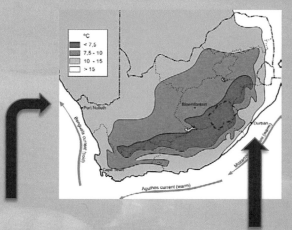

Place: Port Nolloth,
Location: Atlantic Ocean
Average temperature:14.1°C
Annual rainfall: 61mm/year

Types of aquatic life: fish are darker, more brown or silver in colour in order to camouflage themselves against larger predators. There are also more poisonous fish here like the stone fish and the lionfish.

Place: Durban
Location: Indian Ocean
Average temperature: 20.5°C
Average rainfall: 1000mm/year

Types of fish: Brightly coloured, tropical fish. Also fish that are more likely to live symbiotically.

A red crab of the Indian Ocean

Activity Notes:

You can experiment with making two solutions of water, one with lots of salt. Add food dye to one of them and see how they mix.

33

علّمنا منطق الطير

34

8. Communication of Animals

بِسْمِ اللهِ الرَّحْمٰنِ الرَّحِيْمِ

وَوَرِثَ سُلَيْمٰنُ دَاوٗدَ وَقَالَ يٰٓاَيُّهَا النَّاسُ عُلِّمْنَا مَنْطِقَ الطَّيْرِ وَاُوْتِيْنَا مِنْ كُلِّ شَيْءٍ ۗ اِنَّ هٰذَا لَهُوَ الْفَضْلُ الْمُبِيْنُ ﴿١٦﴾

"And Sulaiman inherited Dawud's heir. He said: "O my people! We have been taught the speech of the birds."
The Ant 27:16

حَتّٰٓى اِذَآ اَتَوْا عَلٰى وَادِ النَّمْلِ ۙ قَالَتْ نَمْلَةٌ يٰٓاَيُّهَا النَّمْلُ ادْخُلُوْا مَسٰكِنَكُمْ ۚ لَا يَحْطِمَنَّكُمْ سُلَيْمٰنُ وَجُنُوْدُهٗ ۙ وَهُمْ لَا يَشْعُرُوْنَ ﴿١٨﴾

"Till, when they reached the Valley of the Ants, an ant exclaimed:
O ants! Enter your dwellings lest Solomon and his armies crush
you, unperceiving." The Ant 27:18

فَمَكَثَ غَيْرَ بَعِيْدٍ فَقَالَ اَحَطْتُّ بِمَا لَمْ تُحِطْ بِهٖ وَجِئْتُكَ مِنْ سَبَاٍ بِنَبَاٍ يَّقِيْنٍ ﴿٢٢﴾

"But the Hoopoe stayed not long and said, "I have encompassed
(in knowledge) that which you have not encompassed, and I have
come to you from Sheba with certain news." The Ant 27:22

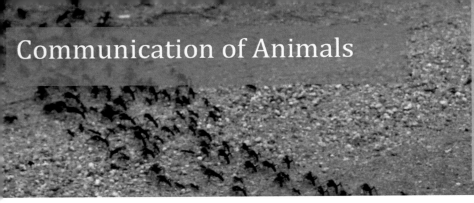

Communication of Animals

Then, when they reached the Valley of the Ants, an ant said: "Ants! Enter your dwellings, so that Sulaiman (Solomon) and his troops do not crush you unknowingly." (The Ants: 18)

Humans have the ability to speak, to form words and sentences. This leads to the ability to think which is how people are able to build cities and have advanced societies. Communication brings man from an isolated being to part of a whole society.

Animals also have their own communication but they use different ways, from sound waves to chemical interactions. Even our pets seem to communicate with us and some people seem able to tune in to what they may be saying. Ants are particularly interesting:

News report: Ants take on slaves to build their nest!

Studies of ant society show there are ants with different jobs like worker ants, soldier ants, and the nursery ants. Studies have also shown that they have the ability to solve complex problems! There are a lot of differences between types of ants from more basic species who hunt through sight alone to more developed ones that have more complex society.

Some species (such as Tetramorium caespitum) attack and take over neighbouring ant colonies. Others are less expansionist, but just as aggressive; they invade colonies to steal eggs or larvae, which they either eat or raise as workers or slaves. Extreme specialists among these slave-raiding ants, such as the Amazon ants, are incapable of feeding themselves and need captured workers to survive. Captured workers of the enslaved species Temnothorax have evolved a counter strategy, destroying just the female pupae of the slave-making Protomognathus Americanus, but sparing the males (who don't take part in slave-raiding as adults).

But on the whole ants are very nice and fun to watch.

Modern day research proves that ants have ways that they can communicate with each other. Even though a single ant is so small, only 2-3mm long, studies have shown that around 500,000 nerve cells are squeezed into their bodies! An ant communicates by releasing chemicals (pheromones) that alert all the nearby ants. The newly alerted ants will spread the news and the direction in which help should be sent, just as the ant was warning the others in the verse above about the advancing army!

Ants use teamwork to make nests using leaves and other forest materials.

The Story of King Sulaiman عليه السلام and the Ants.

Sulaiman was given the ability to understand the speech of the animals. One day travelling at the head of the army, he heard a small ant warning his fellow ants to quickly hide or be trampled. The ant wondered why a Prophet king with a huge army would destroy a small colony of ants. Sulaiman heard the ant and out of respect for the ants he ordered the army to make a detour around the colony. The ants were very happy.

"But the hoopoe stayed not long and said, "I have encompassed [in knowledge] that which you have not encompassed, and I have come to you from Sheba with certain news."
(The Ant:22)

"And Sulaiman inherited David's heir. He said: "O my people! We have been taught the speech of birds..."
(The Ant: 16)

The Story of King Sulaiman, السلام
Bilqis and the Hoopoe Bird

Sulaiman attended regular meetings with the birds so that he could know what they needed and what was happening far and wide. One day, Sulaiman noticed a long absence of the Hoopoe bird. When the bird finally returned, he informed Sulaiman of a wondrous kingdom to the south. The ruler was a queen who was both beautiful and wise but she and her people worshipped the Sun. Sulaiman at once sent a letter to this queen, Bilqis (or Sheba) inviting her to visit him and to learn about Allah. The Hoopoe bird took the letter. She then prepared a gift for him, of the finest gold and jewels. He sent it back, saying that knowledge of Allah was far greater than material gifts. Sulaiman then prepared an ornate palace for her arrival. After she arrived she saw that he was a Prophet of God and then loved and believed in God. Some reports say that she also became his wife.

Many animals have unique ways to communicate and use patterns, movement and body language, chemicals and seismic vibration – where they stamp on the ground or message through water to alert others. Some animals use ultrasonic sounds like dolphins and whales. You can listen to the sound the dolphin makes and have a look at these different animals, all with very unique ways of communication.

Activity notes:
Can you find out how each of these animals communicates? Look up the honey bee, dolphins, cuttlefish, ocean fish and migratory birds.

سُبْحَانَ الَّذِي خَلَقَ الْأَزْوَاجَ

9. Creation Made in Pairs

بِسْمِ اللهِ الرَّحْمٰنِ الرَّحِيْمِ

وَمِنْ كُلِّ شَيْءٍ خَلَقْنَا زَوْجَيْنِ لَعَلَّكُمْ تَذَكَّرُوْنَ ۞

"Of everything We have created pairs so that you may become mindful
that God is One." (The Scattering Winds: 51:49)

سُبْحٰنَ الَّذِيْ خَلَقَ الْاَزْوَاجَ كُلَّهَا مِمَّا تُنْبِتُ الْاَرْضُ وَمِنْ

اَنْفُسِهِمْ وَمِمَّا لَا يَعْلَمُوْنَ ۞

"Glory to God, Who created in pairs all things that the Earth produces, as
well as their own (human) kind and (other) things of which they have no
knowledge." (Ya Siin 36:36)

Creation in Pairs

Of everything We have created pairs so that you may become mindful that God is One."
(The Scattering Winds: 51:49)

The Qur'an verse is describing how Creation is made on a principle of pairs. If we think of night and day, dark and light, from the very basic building blocks of life, electrons and protons in atoms to pairs of chromosomes found in human and animal cells, everything seems to be in this dynamic of pairing and opposites to form the forces that keep Creation in balance. The Qur'an says it is only Allah Who is One, the Originator of all things, Who does not need an opposite.

Most life on Earth reproduces in pairs with a male and female, from humans, to animals and insects. Plants are interesting because they have male and female aspects contained within the one plant and use various methods by which seeds are scattered to other plants or through self-pollination. Some conifer trees for instance, produce two types of cones on the same tree. One of the cone types gives off pollen (the staminate cone). The other type of cone catches the pollen (the ovulate cone) as long as the wind is moving in the right direction. This means the tree can self-pollinate itself and other surrounding trees.

There is such a spectacular variety of animals and plants that we still do not know how many insect and fish species there are on Earth. Last count was about 925,000 species of insects and 32,100 fish species.

Is all life really in pairs?

The Qur'an verse inspires us to think about this. Scientists tell us that 95% of all animal life reproduces in pairs. There is the other 5%, some of which includes hermaphrodites; animals who, like plants, have both male and female parts. There are even some animals that start off female and become male at some point in their lives. Even single cell organisms, like bacteria reproduce in a binary fission, producing an identical replica of itself.

A circular bacterial chromosome, showing DNA replication proceeding bidirectionally, with two replication forks generated at the "origin". Each half of the chromosome replicated by one replication fork is called a "replichore".

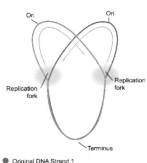

Ori   Ori

Replication fork

Replication fork

Replication fork

Terminus

- Original DNA Strand 1
- Original DNA Strand 2
- New DNA

A male and female pheasant. The males, like most birds, are more flamboyantly decorated than the females.

> "Glory to Him [Allah], Who created all of the pairs that the Earth produces, and their own kind (humans) and other things of that they have no knowledge of."
>
> (Ya-siin:36)

If we look around us, we can see many signs of the pairs in Creation. Even stars come in pairs, with binary stars making up 80% of the massive star population.

The verse above also mentions the things that are not so obvious, that mankind in general has no knowledge of. This could be referring to the unseen world, the world of angelic beings and heavenly realms. It may also be that Allah is allowing us to see, in this day and age, that there is matter and anti-matter. For every particle in creation, there is an unseen oppositely charged particle.

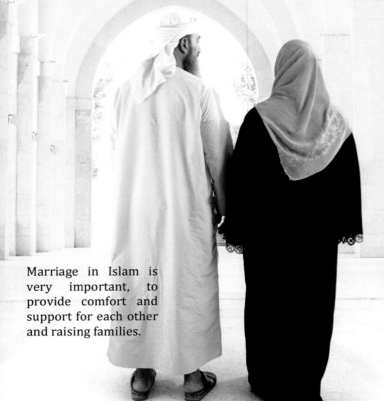

Marriage in Islam is very important, to provide comfort and support for each other and raising families.

Humans as a unique creation

The Qur'an refers to the creation of Humans as something very unique in the Universe. In traditional teachings in Islam, we are taught that we have a Heavenly existence and a worldly existence. When these two realities are united then we begin to reach perfection as a human being. This is yet another aspect of pairing, that of our worldly self and our higher self.

Do the planets come in pairs? In terms of size there is Jupiter and Saturn, Earth and Venus, Neptune and Uranus, Mars and Mercury and Pluto and Eris.

Matter and Antimatter

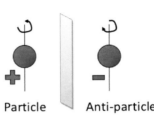

Particle   Anti-particle

In the extremely tiny world of particles, far smaller than atoms, there are quarks and anti-quarks, electrons and positrons and protons and anti-protons. Every particle in the Universe is balanced by its opposite. An antiparticle is like a mirror image of the other. They have the same mass but have an opposite charge and spins in the opposite direction. When these two oppositely charged particles collide, in certain conditions, they annihilate. We can see the symmetry of nature to its most fundamental and smallest point.

Activity Notes:

Think about the opposites we find in nature; day and night, sun and moon, winter and summer and imagine what they symbolise? Also, hold up a small mirror, imagine what you see in the reflection appearing in space on the other side. This is like the hidden world of anti matter.

41

من الظلمات الى النور

10. Destiny and Epigenetics

بِسْمِ اللهِ الرَّحْمٰنِ الرَّحِيْمِ

مَآ أَصَابَ مِنْ مُّصِيْبَةٍ فِي الْأَرْضِ وَلَا فِيْ أَنْفُسِكُمْ إِلَّا فِيْ كِتٰبٍ مِّنْ قَبْلِ أَنْ نَّبْرَأَهَا ۚ إِنَّ ذٰلِكَ عَلَى اللهِ يَسِيْرٌ ۝

"Nothing occurs, either in the earth or in yourselves, that was not set down in writing before We brought it into being–that is easy for Allah" (Al-Hadid 57:22)

الٓرٰ ۚ كِتٰبٌ أَنْزَلْنٰهُ إِلَيْكَ لِتُخْرِجَ النَّاسَ مِنَ الظُّلُمٰتِ إِلَى النُّوْرِ ۚ بِإِذْنِ رَبِّهِمْ إِلٰى صِرَاطِ الْعَزِيْزِ الْحَمِيْدِ ۝

"Alif, Lam, Ra. [This is] a Book which We have revealed to you, [O Muhammad], that you might bring mankind out of darkness into the light by permission of their Lord - to the path of the Exalted in Might, the Praiseworthy" (Abraham 14:1)

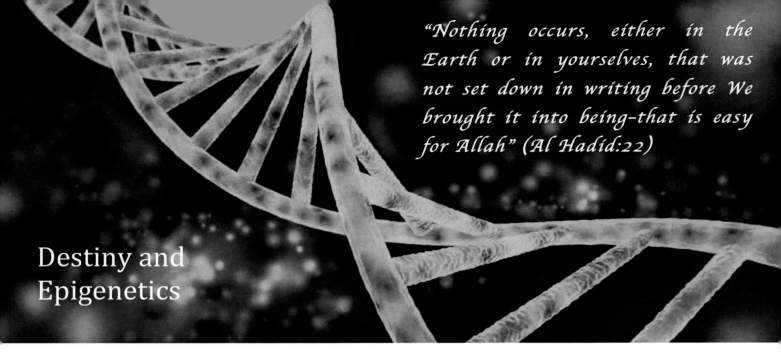

Destiny and Epigenetics

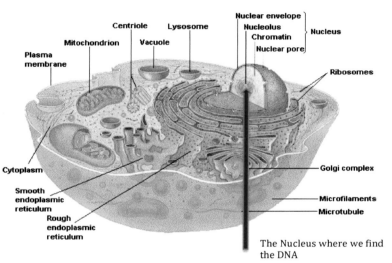

The Nucleus where we find the DNA

In your body there are about 10 trillion cells, each extremely complex, and within each of these cells there is a nucleus and within that is the DNA and your genetic code. The DNA strands are extremely fine and extremely long; amazingly, all the DNA in your body would stretch to the sun and back four times. This shows one aspect of the incredible nature of how we are made as humans.

DNA or your genomes, have all the information your body needs to function, make more cells and each cell knows, because of Methal groups, what cell function to manifest. The Methal group switches on and off the Genome. Histones, which are proteins, are more like knobs then switches. They control how much each gene is expressed, depending on how tightly wound the Histone allows. So the Genome (DNA) is the hardware, and the epigenome is like the software, telling the DNA what to do. Each of our tendencies is imprinted on our genetic code and can be passed down to our children.

Imagine there are some twins. They were separated at birth and have the same genetic code. They ended up following very different lifestyles and as a consequence, twin one has a different gene code operating then his twin brother. Why is that? In the science of Epigenetics (literally above genetics), we find the different gene codes become activated or recessed according to lifestyle choice and external factors. ***The decisions we take and the actions we do can literally change our genetic code.***

Studies have shown for instance that when the protective chemical that seals the gene becomes frayed due to stress and anxiety, the gene stops producing a healing code and a person may develop serious illnesses like cancer and mental disorders. If, on the other hand, people adopt a healthier and more positive lifestyle, then their genes become more effective and they are much less likely to get a serious disease, even if it is in their genetic code.

So is our destiny fixed? Perhaps our *potential* destinies are all written into our DNA code "...set down in writing."(57:22) but with the gift of free will, we can either become our best or worst versions of ourselves.

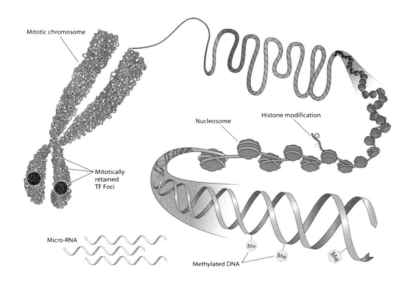

Do Our Actions Really Affect Our Genetic Code?

"A Book We have sent down to you so that you may bring forth mankind from the darkness into the light..." (14:1)

From an Islamic perspective, how we act very much depends on what we believe. The Qur'an differentiates between those who lead a good, peaceful life and those who do not, to help encourage people to choose good actions. The Qur'an describes 'believers' and 'unbelievers' - those who believe in God and those who do not. Perhaps you may think the belief is just in their minds but it goes deeper than that. The Qur'an does not say "they *think* they are believers" but refers to them as "The believers" that is because they literally are, they have become, possibly even changing their genetic code as epigenetics seems to suggest, so that they are a believer, down to each cell. Everything that they think and do is in relation to that belief and the same applies for those who do not believe. People behave very differently depending on what they believe, people literally become who they are and what they are doing and even thinking, so be careful! Thankfully, God is very Merciful, as Muslims believe, and always offers everyone a way out, a chance to renew their faith and belief in God, choosing light, kindness, selflessness and goodness as part of their everyday life.

Imagine this case study of Twin 1 and Twin 2:
Identical twins who followed very different life choices.

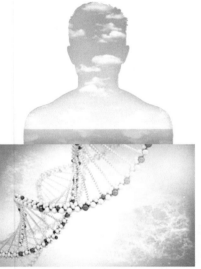

Here we have the inner life of twin number one. He ignored all the good advice, choosing to cheat and lie his way to make money. His life is full of stress and fear for loosing his riches and has very few real friends. He turns to entertainments to make him feel better. He is less handsome than his twin because of all the bad thoughts he has. He developed cancer in his 50's.

Here we have the inner life of twin two, who has tried his best to follow a good life, being kind, patient and generous. He has made a lot of money but gives a lot to charity. He is someone who has followed recommendations from the Qur'an, and of the Holy Prophet. He experiences life in full richness and is happy and faces life's challenges with a positive attitude throughout his life.

News Report: Being a Muslim Can Seriously Affect Your Health!

Are Muslims really healthier and happier? If we look at worldwide statistics*, People in Muslim countries (over 90% Muslim population) are much less likely (31% less) to develop cancer than in countries that are mostly non-Muslim. The statistics show that people in Muslim countries are much healthier and less likely to develop cancer.

This could be because the Prophet Muhammad ﷺ recommended many things to have a healthy way of life including:

Fasting Ramadan – clears the system of toxins
Regular prayers – removes stress and anxiety
Not over-eating – leaves room for a healthy digestion
Not over sleeping – waking for early morning prayer
Pinch of salt before and after meals – aids digestion
And many more healthy daily habits...

*Cancer research UK, Wikipedia: WHO, Guardian article Muslim

Did you know that Holy people's bodies do not decompose after they die? That is one of the signs of the Saints and Prophets. Their genetic code must be quite special!

What is the Muslim code of conduct? It says in Qur'an to Love, be kind, forgive others, be generous, give charity, pray, accept that all good and bad comes from God, avoid drinking alcohol and doing things that damage your health, be clean, eat good food but eat little, be just and fair, be honest, be humble. Of all the amazing things we have seen so far, the greatest miracle, Muslims believe, is the ability of the Qur'an to change hearts from darkness to light.

Activity Notes:

Think of a really kind thing that you can do for someone else; your parents, a teacher, a friend perhaps.

فَإِنَّا لَمُوسِعُونَ

11. Earth's Protective Atmosphere

بِسْمِ اللهِ الرَّحْمٰنِ الرَّحِيمِ

وَجَعَلْنَا السَّمَآءَ سَقْفًا مَّحْفُوظًا ۖ وَّهُمْ عَنْ اٰيٰتِهَا مُعْرِضُونَ ۝

"And We made the sky a protected ceiling, but they, from its signs, turn away."
(The Prophets 21:32)

Earth's Protective Atmosphere

"And We made the sky a protected ceiling, but they are turning away from its signs." (Surat Al-Anbiya:32)

Earth's atmosphere is an extraordinary system that perfectly allows life to flourish. We are able to live far away from the extreme cold of space, the intense sunbursts and harmful radiation that would wipe out all life in a pocket of sunshine and breathable air. Earth's atmosphere also protects us from thousands of meteors raining down from space. Without it, we would not even feel the warmth of the sun. How remarkable it is, that what appears to be gaseous air, combined with the inherent structure of the Earth, creates such a unique and delicate system of life? Indeed, it seems very much like the "protected ceiling" as the Qur'an says.

Thermosphere and Exosphere
These regions eventually end at 10,000km above sea level, merging with outer space that has no atmosphere. Molecules here are very rare. In the thermosphere, they may travel 1km before they collide with another. Molecules can heat up to extreme temperatures of thousands of degrees but because they are so 'spaced out', they would not feel hot to a travelling astronaut.

Jetstream & Stratosphere
Airplanes and jet planes often fly in this zone because it's very stable. This is where the Ozone layer exists that protects us from harmful UV radiations from the sun, yet allowing beneficial rays that are essential to life.

Temperatures: -270 C, -85, 0

Distance from Earths surface: 690km, 85, 50, 20

Mesosphere
Here asteroids enter the atmosphere and are burned up. Asteroids travel at great speeds and when they enter the dense atmosphere, the speed produces friction, which then heats up the rock or metal until it vaporises! If this didn't happen, millions of meteors (many only a few centimetres across) would hit the Earth every day.

Troposphere
This is where the air we breathe and all the weather happens, this is a beautifully protected shell around the

Earth so that there is constant mild weather and no extreme heats or colds. Even though it may seem very cold sometimes or very hot this is nothing compared to the extremes you find on other planets in our system...

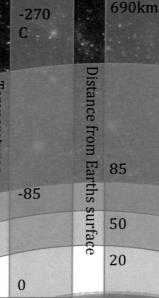

Atmospheres on other planets

Tired of the weather on Earth? Perhaps try another planet in our system....

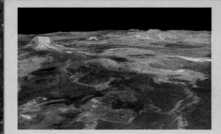

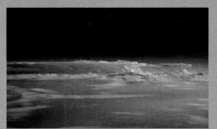

Mars is the nearest planet, but has a very thin poisonous atmosphere, mostly of Nitrogen. You would find it very cold, as low as -82 degrees c. There is no protective shell, so meteorites hit the surface regularly. Dust storms can cover the entire planet in a couple of days. But Mars does have rocky terrain, craters and caves that makes it interesting to explore.

Venus has a surface temperature of 467 degrees c and is surrounded by clouds of sulphuric acid as well as an unbreathable atmosphere of 96% carbon dioxide. Venus rotates extremely rapidly so that the winds are 300 mph. You would also be crushed under the extreme pressure which is 92 times stronger than Earth's.

Without an actual surface, Neptune would be hard to even land on. The gaseous atmosphere is mostly composed of methane with huge quantities of methane, ammonia and ammonium ices. Temperatures are just above that of space about -240 degrees c. Being 4,495km from the sun, the sun would appear like a small dot.

Earth's Protective Magnetic Shield

As well as the atmospheric protection, Earth also has a huge magnetic shield reaching 100's of thousands of kilometres into space. This, extremely effectively, wards away lethal fiery bursts from the sun.

There needs to be a 2,700-degree F (1,500C) difference between the inner core and the mantle to spur "thermal movements" that, along with Earth's spin, create the magnetic field. The very heart of our planet is a solid inner core of mostly iron that is about the size of the moon. It is so hot (about 5000°C to 7200°C) that its temperature equals that of the "surface" of the sun, but it remains solid because of the combined pressure of everything above it being pulled towards it by gravity.

The difference in temperature between the inner core and the mantle causes the Earth to become a giant magnet.

Energy Bursts from the Sun

The energy transmitted in just one of these bursts detected in recent years, was calculated to be equivalent to 100 billion atomic bombs. Fifty-eight hours after the burst, it was observed that the magnetic needles of compasses displayed unusual movement and 250 kilometers above the Earth's atmosphere, the temperature suddenly increased to 2,500°C.

Homework Notes

Magnet experiment.
Order some iron filings and a magnet online and experiment with them. Remember to keep the iron filings in a bag because they stick fast to the magnet! Also, you could put some food dye in some water and run it past a magnet in water; does it change course? Can you recreate the effect that the Earth has?

كُلٌّ فِي فَلَكٍ يَسْبَحُونَ

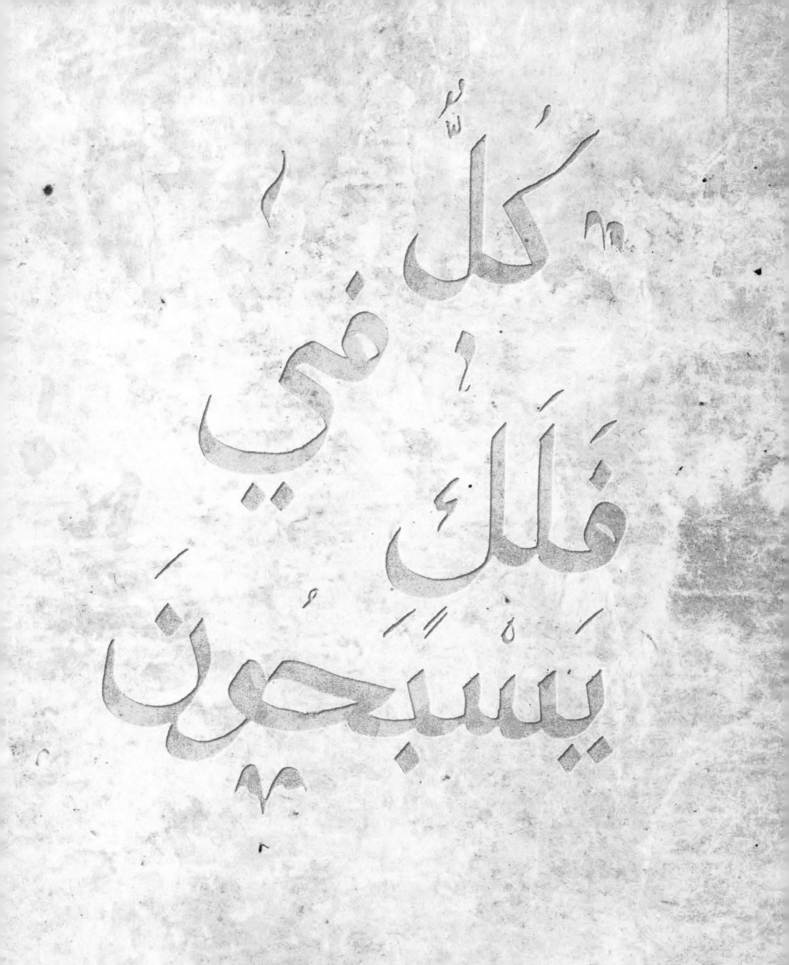

12. Orbit & Speed of Light

بِسْمِ اللهِ الرَّحْمٰنِ الرَّحِيْمِ

وَهُوَ الَّذِيْ خَلَقَ الَّيْلَ وَ النَّهَارَ وَ الشَّمْسَ وَ الْقَمَرَ ۖ كُلٌّ فِيْ فَلَكٍ يَّسْبَحُوْنَ ۝

"And He is the One who created night and the day, the Sun and the Moon; each floating in its orbit."
(The Prophets 21:33)

اَلشَّمْسُ وَ الْقَمَرُ بِحُسْبَانٍ ۝

"The Sun and Moon (move) by precise calculation."
(The All-Merciful 55:5)

يُدَبِّرُ الْاَمْرَ مِنَ السَّمَآءِ اِلَى الْاَرْضِ ثُمَّ يَعْرُجُ اِلَيْهِ فِيْ يَوْمٍ كَانَ مِقْدَارُهٗٓ اَلْفَ سَنَةٍ مِّمَّا تَعُدُّوْنَ ۝

"(Allah) regulates the Cosmic affair from the heavens to the earth; then shall it ascend to Him in one day the measure of which is a thousand years of what you count."
(The Prostration 32:5)

Orbit

"It is He who created night and day, the Sun and the Moon, each floating in its orbit."
[The Prophets:33]

It is astonishing that almost 1500 years ago, there was specific mention of the orbits of the Sun and the Moon in the Qur'an.

An illustration of the Istanbul observatory in 1577

Several centuries ago, it was generally accepted in the West that the Earth was flat. Philosophers also used to think that the Earth was the centre of the Solar System and the Universe. In the 16th Century Renaissance, Nicolas Copernicus put forward his theory that the Solar System was moving in orbits around the Sun. Galileo Galilei also continued this work, which greatly upset the religious authorities as they found these theories to be heretical (against faith in God) and Galileo spent the rest of his life under house arrest. Galileo would have been better off in a Muslim country where orbits had been accepted for over one thousand years! In fact, Galileo studied astronomical texts from Muslim astronomers, one of whom, Al-Buruni, explored ideas about our rotating planet 600 years before.

What is gravity?

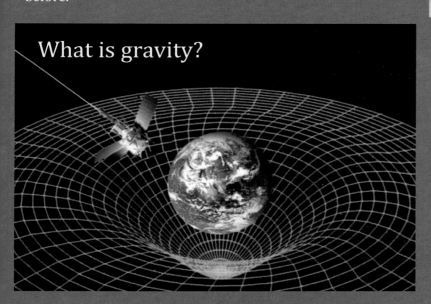

There would not be orbits without gravity. Gravity positions everything as we see it in the Universe, creating the orbits around one body and another.

Sir Isaac Newton was the first scientist to discover the law of gravity in 1687 when an apple landed on his head! Albert Einstein then refined it in 1915 with his general theory of relativity. He believed that these huge objects actually bend the space-time field to produce a force that then attracts other objects towards it. The objects in effect, then 'roll around' in the curvature produced by the gravitational field as illustrated here.

A new theory of gravity is currently being researched which suggests that there is actually a black hole or a singularity at the centre of every object including the galaxies, stars, planets, as well as atoms. This black hole, produced by the spin, holds the objects together with an opposite force preventing the collapse of the object.

Speed of Light

Another amazing example of the precise nature of the orbits can be found when examining this verse, "He arranges (each) matter from the Heaven to the Earth: then it will ascend to Him a distance in one Day, at a measure of which is a thousand years of those which you count." This Qur'anic verse describes Allah's arrangement of every matter (everything) from the Heavens to the Earth and then describes that the matter travels back to Him. It then describes a measure and time. Islamic scholars have been astonished that if this is worked out as follows, *an exact prediction of the speed of light is made.*

The speed of light is the distance travelled by light in 1 second and can be calculated as: SPEED = DISTANCE/TIME = 299792.458km/second. From the Qur'anic verse shown above this speed is given as "the cosmic affair" which "travels to Him a distance in one Day, at a measure of one thousand years of what you count."

What is it that we count? From time immemorial we have always counted the phases of the Moon to indicate the passing of time. In the Islamic tradition, there are 12 lunar cycles for each Islamic year, where each lunar cycle corresponds to a specific Islamic month.

How do we measure this? The measure of this counting system can be taken as the distance the Moon travels in one lunar month (2,150,000 km*) multiplied by 12 to make a lunar year. The overall distance that we measure is thus given as: Measure of distance = 12 x d = 12 x 2,150,000 km = 25,800,000 km, where d = 2,150,000 km, is the approximate distance the Moon travels in one complete orbit. So "one thousand years of what you count" is the DISTANCE in our equation and is given as: DISTANCE = Measure of distance x 1000 = 25,800,000 x 1000 = 25,800,000,000

What is **TIME** in our equation? "... this affair travels to him a distance in one day ..." therefore the TIME can be given as: TIME = 1 day = 1 x 24 hours x 60 minutes x 60 seconds = 86,400 seconds

Speed of Light The speed of light, c, can therefore be calculated as: C=SPEED=DISTANCE/TIME=25,800,000,000/86,400=299,000 km/s. This is within 0.4% of the true value, where any discrepancy is most likely due to the approximate nature of the values for distance. Speed of light according to the British National Physics lab is 299,792.459 km/s.

* The standard distance given is 2,415,621km, however this assumes a static orbit. The value 2,150,000 is more exact as it takes into account the helical nature of the orbit.

Have a look at the beautiful patterns below discovered recently by scientist John Martineaux. These are the orbital patterns of each planet in the Solar System in their relative position to the Earth. The patterns of their positions are charted every few days. Over 7 or 8 years, these wonderful patterns emerge.

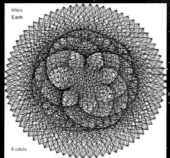
Mars
Earth
8 orbits

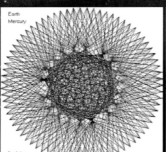
Earth
Mercury
6 orbits

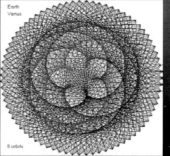
Earth
Venus
8 orbits

Moon (move) by precise calculations." From the beginning of our time on Earth, Humankind has used the passing of the Sun and the Moon to track time and the stars to navigate around the globe. These heavenly bodies provide an exact and accurate way to measure time and place that we still use today. Would time seem to exist without the movement of the Sun and the Moon?

"He (Allah) arranges [each] matter from the Heaven to the Earth; then it will ascend to Him a distance in one Day, at a measure of which is a thousand years of those which you count. "
(The Prostration:5)

Activity notes:

1. How long would it take for you to send a message travelling at the speed of light to your friend on planet Pluto, 7.5 billion km away?

2. <u>Dance of the planets</u>
With a group of children, let them choose a planet, moon or the Sun and make a version of this with art materials. Then organise the children to 'orbit' each other according to the solar system. Playing suitable music to accompany.

والسماء ذات الحبك

13. The Universe, Black Holes and Pulsar Stars

بِسْمِ اللهِ الرَّحْمٰنِ الرَّحِيمِ

اِنَّمَآ اَمْرُهٗٓ اِذَآ اَرَادَ شَيْـًٔا اَنْ يَّقُوْلَ لَهٗ كُنْ فَيَكُوْنُ ۝

"Whenever He decides to create something He has only to say, "Be!" and it comes into existence." (Ya Siin 36:82)

فَلَآ اُقْسِمُ بِمَوٰقِعِ النُّجُوْمِ ۝

"I swear by the falling of stars, it is a great oath if you knew, it is a Noble Qur'an." (The Event 56:75)

ثُمَّ اسْتَوٰٓى اِلَى السَّمَآءِ وَهِىَ دُخَانٌ فَقَالَ لَهَا وَلِلْاَرْضِ ائْتِيَا

طَوْعًا اَوْ كَرْهًا ۚ قَالَتَآ اَتَيْنَا طَآئِعِيْنَ ۝ .

"He established His dominance over the sky, which (for that time) was like smoke. Then He told the Heavens and the Earth, 'Take your shape either willingly or by force.' They said, 'We do come willingly'."
(Explained in Detail 41:11)

وَالسَّمَآءَ بَنَيْنٰهَا بِاَيْدٍ وَّاِنَّا لَمُوْسِعُوْنَ ۝

"And We have built the sky with a mighty power and verily We are expanding it." (Drivers of the Winds 51:47)

اَلنَّجْمُ الثَّاقِبُ ۝   وَمَآ اَدْرٰىكَ مَا الطَّارِقُ ۝   وَالسَّمَآءِ وَالطَّارِقِ ۝

"By the Heavens and the Morning Star (al-Tariq), How will you comprehend what al-Tariq is? It is a piercing star." (Al-Tariq 86: 1-3)

The Universe

"And We have built the sky with a mighty power and verily We are expanding it." (Ahd-Dhariyat:47)

"Then He directed Himself to the Heaven when it was smoke, and then said to it and to Earth: 'Come willingly or by force', they said, 'We do come willingly.'" (Fussilat – 11)

"Whenever He decides to create something He has only to say, "Exist," and it comes into existence". (Ya Siin:82)

Scientists generally agree that the Universe was created in an instant at the time of the Big Bang. Initially after the inflation, a smoke-like vapour appeared and within seconds condensed into more and more particles. Scientists can see with extra powerful telescopes all the way back in time (because the speed of light is within limits) so all information about the history of the observable Universe can be seen right now. Scientists have confirmed that the Universe seems to have been expanding ever since the initial 'Big Bang' and will continue to do so.

In the Qur'an, it says "And We have built the sky with a mighty power and verily We are expanding it." This is an extraordinary description from the Ancient Book.

In this verse, the Qur'an describes the Heaven as smoke, or vapour and how Earth came from this. Pictured below is a timeline of the possible stages of Earth's formation. Some astrophysicists believe that about 4.6 billion years ago, a gaseous nebula collapsed due to gravity, first forming the Sun, and then through the clumping together of the remaining materials – the planets. The Moon is thought to have emerged when a small planet collided with the early Earth. Eventually the Earth stabilised and cooled. Water was formed and life began. And Allah knows best.

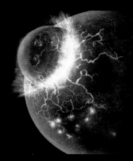

The Birth of Stars

From the remains, new stars arise.

How are stars made?

Deep within the gigantic interstellar clouds, which are produced after a supernova, huge regions of gas and dust can begin to collapse under their own gravity. As the cloud collapses, the material at the center begins to heat up. This early star is known as a Protostar, this will one day become a star.

The dust and debris left behind by novae and supernovae eventually blend with the surrounding interstellar gas and dust, enriching it with the heavy elements and chemical compounds produced during stellar explosions. Eventually, those materials are recycled, providing the building blocks for a new generation of stars and accompanying planetary systems.

"I swear by the falling of stars, it is a great oath if you knew, it is a Noble Quran." (The Event:75)

Black Holes and Pulsar Stars

Supernovae Leave Behind Neutron Stars or Black Holes

Main sequence stars over eight solar masses are destined to die in a titanic explosion called a supernova. In a supernova, the star's core collapses and then explodes. The star no longer has any way to support its own mass, and the iron core collapses. In just a matter of seconds, the core shrinks from roughly 7000 km across to just a dozen, and the temperature reaches 100 billion degrees or more.

Neutron Stars
If the collapsing stellar core at the center of a supernova contains between about 1.4 and 3 solar masses, the collapse continues until electrons and protons combine to form neutrons, producing a neutron star. Because it contains so much mass packed into such a small volume, the gravitation at the surface of a neutron star is immense.

Neutron stars are incredibly dense – the same as the density of an atomic nucleus.

Neutron stars also produce huge beams of radiation that sweep around the star like a beam from a lighthouse. These neutron stars are called pulsar stars and can produce a curious knocking sound that can be detected by instruments on Earth. In the Qur'an there is a verse that could be describing this sound, as the word 'tariq' (tawariq) means 'knocker'. Could this be what the Qur'an is referring to?

"By the Heavens and al-Tariq. How will you comprehend what al-Tariq is? It is a piercing star." (Al-Tariq 1-3)

What is inside a Black Hole?

No matter can escape from a black hole. It draws in everything around it including stars and galaxies. Astrophysicists now believe there is a supermassive black hole at the centre of every galaxy. When an object approaches a black hole it reaches the 'event horizon', once this horizon is crossed, nothing can escape. An object would appear to be stretched out eternally. Some scientists think that within a black hole there could be a 'wormhole', a link to another place and time in space!

"I swear by the falling of stars, it is a great oath if you knew, it is a Noble Quran." (The Event:75)

In the verse above, the Qur'an describes the 'falling of stars'. We may first think of a falling star that we see at night, but actually these are comets passing near our atmosphere. The Qur'an may be describing a star falling in on itself, or in other words, collapsing.

How big can stars get?
Stars like our Sun are tiny in comparison to some of the really massive stars! Have a look at Arcturus, an orange giant star in the Bootes constellation, it is the brightest star in the Northern Hemisphere.
Sirius is the brightest of all the stars. It is a binary star with a white dwarf known as Sirius 'B'. Sirius is one of the closest stars to Earth and is 25 times more luminous than our sun.

Homework Notes
The knocking sound of the pulsar stars sound strange to listen to: Look up online for this sound.

إن الله عز حكمتم

58

14. Particle Physics

بِسْمِ اللهِ الرَّحْمٰنِ الرَّحِيمِ

وَمَا تَكُونُ فِي شَأْنٍ وَمَا تَتْلُوا مِنْهُ مِن قُرْءَانٍ وَلَا تَعْمَلُونَ مِنْ عَمَلٍ إِلَّا كُنَّا عَلَيْكُمْ
شُهُودًا إِذْ تُفِيضُونَ فِيهِ وَمَا يَعْزُبُ عَن رَّبِّكَ مِن مِّثْقَالِ ذَرَّةٍ فِي الْأَرْضِ وَلَا فِي السَّمَاءِ
وَلَا أَصْغَرَ مِن ذَلِكَ وَلَا أَكْبَرَ إِلَّا فِي كِتَابٍ مُّبِينٍ ﴿٦١﴾

"... Not even an atom's weight eludes your Lord, either on Earth or in Heaven. Nor is there anything smaller than that, or larger, which is not in a Clear Book. (Yunus, 10:61)

وَالسَّمَاءِ ذَاتِ الْحُبُكِ ﴿٧﴾

إِنَّكُمْ لَفِي قَوْلٍ مُّخْتَلِفٍ ﴿٨﴾

"I swear by the Sky and its numerous strings, you are certainly at variance with each other concerning the truth"
(ahd-Dhanyat 51:7-8)

وَالْخَيْلَ وَالْبِغَالَ وَالْحَمِيرَ لِتَرْكَبُوهَا وَزِينَةً وَيَخْلُقُ مَا لَا تَعْلَمُونَ ﴿٨﴾

"...and He creates other things beyond your knowledge."
(The Bees 16:8)

وَلَوْ أَنَّمَا فِي الْأَرْضِ مِن شَجَرَةٍ أَقْلَامٌ وَالْبَحْرُ يَمُدُّهُ مِن بَعْدِهِ سَبْعَةُ أَبْحُرٍ مَّا
نَفِدَتْ كَلِمَاتُ اللَّهِ إِنَّ اللَّهَ عَزِيزٌ حَكِيمٌ ﴿٢٧﴾

"And if whatever trees upon the Earth were pens and the sea [was ink], replenished thereafter by seven [more] seas, the words of Allah would not be exhausted. Indeed, Allah is Exalted in Might and Wise."
(Luqman 31:27)

Particle Physics

"... Not even an atom's weight eludes your Lord, either on Earth or in Heaven. Nor is there anything smaller than that, or larger, which is not in a Clear Book." (Yunus, 10:61)

The Tiny World of Quantum Particles

Scientists used to think that the atom was the smallest thing that there is, after all, in a grain of sand 1mm across there are approximately 8 million trillion (8,000,000,000,000,000) atoms, so how can we imagine smaller?

The Qur'an mentions things smaller than atoms and indeed, in the 1930's, physicists discovered the existence of a group of particles much smaller than atoms. These particles are believed to form the physical fabric of everything that we see. From the verse above, we may conclude that the Qur'an could be referring to these tiny, tiny particles.

The undescribable

Time

Everything we know

We now know that there are electrons, protons and neutrons that form the atom. Going even tinier there are quarks, neutrinos and other quantum particles such as Planck particles, which are measured at the Planck scale of $1.6 \times 10-35$. The Planck length is theoretically the smallest measurement in existence, although it is too small to be successfully measured. If you compare the same grain of sand, but this time to the size of the entire Universe, that is the difference between the atom and the Planck particle.

The Universe at these tiny scales is not immediately observable. In this tiny universe, vibrations actually create the forms that we see. Vibrations or frequencies are everywhere. Some things we can see like a rainbow. These are the different frequencies of colour.

New theories of these particles describe them as existing in an ether-like sea, as Einstein had predicted, where each particle sends out a resonance, interacting and affecting other particles, like pebbles being dropped into water, each with their own characteristics.

Here we have a diagram of the waves and frequencies. Some things like visible light we can see ourselves but other frequencies can be only experienced indirectly, such as a radio frequency or x-rays that are detected using special instruments. All matter can be said to be operating at one frequency or another, but we may not be able to directly observe it. In some cases, like that of sound vibrations being passed through sand and water, patterns may emerge revealing its presence indirectly.

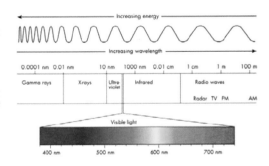

The 'big picture' in both science and Qur'an shows that we experience only a small portion of everything that is going on.

In the spiritual world, the Holy Prophet ﷺ described how he travelled to all the Seven Heavens in his Night Journey. In order to give a description of something that was indescribable, he used examples of precious stones. For instance, the First Heaven was made of red ruby, the second of red coral, others of copper, white pearl, red gold until pure light in the Seventh Heaven. Different angels reside in the different Heavens and each has its purpose. Paradise is said to be located in the first Heaven. Why are there Seven Heavens rather than just one? The Holy Prophet ﷺ was very specific about this. There must be mysteries, far greater than we can imagine.

"...and He creates other things beyond your knowledge." (16:8)

"And if whatever trees upon the Earth were pens and the sea [was ink], replenished thereafter by seven [more] seas, the Words of Allah would not be exhausted. Indeed, Allah is Exalted in Might and Wisdom."

(Surat Luqman:27)

How much can we imagine?

Understanding the mysteries of the Universe requires a great deal of intelligence, imagination and insight. In the verse above, Allah says that His Knowledge is endless, unlike our knowledge. He says if all the seas were ink and the trees were pens that His Knowledge will never end. Allah also refers here to the Seven Heavens as endless oceans (of knowledge).

Scientists have worked out that the normal matter that we can detect and observe is only 4.9% of the Universe. Can we really say we know anything? Even the vast knowledge of all the scientists, all the books in the libraries cannot describe more than 5% of the Universe.

Time

Time is one of the dimensions that we can sense but cannot touch. Time does strange things when an object is travelling at the speed of light...it stretches, so that the object never goes faster than the speed of light. In fact, when an object approaches the speed of light it becomes increasingly large so that you would need increasing force to push the object along, up to infinite velocity – impossible! This is because of the relationship between mass, velocity, energy and the speed of light. Both mass and energy become infinite when approaching the speed of light.

Physicists are now looking at time as moments appearing one moment after another. Like slices of bread, but very fine. So fine you cannot notice it.

Everything is in motion

On Earth, we are quite happy living our days standing apparently quite stationary but actually the Earth is spinning at 1,667 km/hour.

Stretch your mind and use your intuition to think about the mysterious of the Universe...Scientists like Einstein understood huge laws of the Universe, not so much by just thinking, but by using his intuition and inspirations.

"The distinction between the past, present and future is only a stubbornly persistent illusion." Albert Einstein

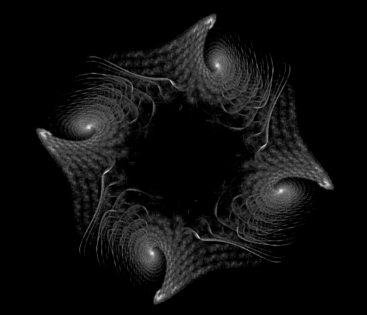

Dark energy and dark matter take up 95.1% of the Universe

Everything else is what we can see and measure. Dark matter and dark energy are really mysterious and vast aspects of the Universe. According to scientists, dark matter makes up 26.8% and dark energy is 68.3%. Astrophysicists can only detect dark matter indirectly by examining its gravitational effect on massive objects. They think both dark matter and dark energy help form the Universe, keep the galaxies rotating and actually control the expansion of the Universe. This dark matter may also have an effect on how the Universe is structured with some astrophysicists describing it as cosmic strings. This is similar to the verse in Qu'ran that says:

"I swear by the Sky and its numerous strings, you are certainly at variance with each other concerning the truth" (ahd-Dhanyat 51:7-8)

The Prophet Muhammad ﷺ lived almost 1500 years ago. He was born in 570 A.D - a time when houses were made of earth, there was no electricity, messages were carried by horseback and medicine was primitive. Around this time in the rest of the world, the Roman, Byzantine and Persian Empires as well as the Tang Dynasty in China were all flourishing. In England, the Romans had left and people were in the midst of the Dark Ages with the legendary King Arthur advising his Knights at the Round Table.

When Prophet Muhammad ﷺ was born, Mecca was a small town in the desert that drew pilgrims to visit the Kaaba, which was built by the Prophet Abraham long before. It was a primitive society in many ways; people would worship idols and have an undeveloped sense of morality and human rights.

Imagine how within the short life of the Prophet Muhammad ﷺ, he came to be the most esteemed among men? His message brought social equality, rights for women, emancipation of slaves, fair trials and social order as well as practical and successful spiritual practices leading to happiness, inner peace and enlightenment. His name ﷺ still brings tears of love to the faithful.

Something that so impressed the people of his time was the great depth of his knowledge. There are many well-recorded hadith (sayings of the Prophet ﷺ) that show his ability to foresee events. The Prophet also had great intuitive knowledge of everyone he met and also brought knowledge about the use of plants and diet for medical treatments. His advice forms the basis of the huge advances seen in the history of Muslim medicine.

In a well-authenticated hadith, Imam Ahmad narrated that Usamah ibn Shuraik (r) said:

"I was with the Prophet ﷺ when the Bedouins came to him and said, 'O Messenger of Allah, should we seek medicine?' He said,'Yes, O servants of Allah, seek medicine, for Allah has not created a disease except that he has also created its cure, except for one illness.' They said, 'And what is that?' He said, 'Old age'."

The Prophet ﷺ would advise the correct plants and treatments for a huge variety of illnesses, physical, psychological and spiritual. The Prophet also prayed for people using verses of the Holy Qur'an as there is also much emphasis on the healing power of the Qur'an. Different verses such as verse 82 in Sura al-Isra (The Night Journey), describes how the Qur'an has been sent down for healing and as a mercy to all people who are willing to believe.

"And We sent down in the Qur'an such things that have healing and mercy for the Believers." (al-Isra 17:82)

"O you who believe! Be in reverential awe of Allah and believe in His Messenger. He will give you twofold of His Mercy and will appoint for you a light wherein you shall walk, and will forgive you, and Allah is Ever-Forgiving, Most Merciful."(57:28)

This glass case contains an actual hair of the Prophet Muhammad. It is a miracle in itself that it still exists as well as other artefacts such as his turban. Human hair generally decomposes within a year, although hair has been found on mummies in extreme dry climates and extreme cold climates where bacteria do not have a chance to get to it. There are many strands of hair of the Holy Prophet treasured by the Muslims and they are not kept in extreme conditions. A reason why the hair does not disintegrate could be because of the Holy nature of the Prophet Muhammad. He is said to be purified to such an extent that he had no coarse matter remaining and was pure light, and light cannot have a shadow. As one of his companions, Hadrat Abdullah ibn Abbas (r) says, "The Holy Prophet had no shadow. His radiance would eclipse even the bright sun. In front of a lighted lamp, His radiance would be more powerful." (iii) One of the signs of an authentic hair of the Prophet, is that it does not cast a shadow.

Muslims believe that Allah revealed to the Holy Prophet knowledge of the unseen that would allow him to see beyond this world and into the Seven Heavens and so he knew how everything was created and sustained. It is documented that the Prophet went on a 'Night Journey' where he came 'two bows length or nearer' to Allah Himself. On this journey he saw all the wonders of Creation in the Heavens and the Earth as it says in Qur'an: "...Certainly, he saw the greatest signs of his Lord." (53:8-18)

It was to Prophet Muhammad that the Holy Qur'an was revealed, with all its wisdom and guidance. Allah refers to the Prophet's tremendous character when He says that if the Qur'an were revealed on a mountain it would be humbled and crushed to pieces out of awe of Allah. "Had We sent down this Qur'an on a mountain, verily you would have seen it humble itself and split asunder for fear of Allah." (59:21)

Roses and pearls have special significance in Islam; pearls representing purity and roses representing the Heavenly scent of Paradise and of the Holy Prophet.

Seekers of Knowledge

It is in the very nature of human beings to search for knowledge and truth. Both scientists and religious people have always wondered at Creation and the secrets of our existence.

In the scientific world, Sir Isaac Newton (1641-1726), one of the Western World's greatest mathematicians, spent 15 years in near isolation in contemplation and research where he discovered the law of gravity. Although he is considered by many as the founder of modern, fact based, materialistic science, he had a firm belief in God and would marvel at the wonders of Creation. Another very famous scientist Max Planck, who founded modern quantum theory, says, *"As a man who has devoted his whole life to the most clear headed science, to the study of matter, I can tell you as a result of my research about atoms this much: There is no matter as such...We must assume behind this force the existence of a conscious and intelligent mind. This mind is the matrix of all matter."* There are many modern physicists like Nassim Harramein, whose research shows that we indeed exist as a unified, conscious whole.

Modern findings in science, especially in quantum physics, are now agreeing more and more with great mystical writers such as Ibn Arabi (1165-1240) who wrote about the nature of existence.

Muslims who are searching for this greater understanding, also spend many hours in contemplation and reflection, often turning to the Qur'an for insight and inspiration. As one of the Companions of Muhammad, Abdullah ibn Masood (r), said about the Qur'an; *"When you intend to acquire knowledge, deeply study the Qur'an for in it lies the [principles] of knowledge of the ancients and future generations."(iv).*

Over the centuries, great thinkers have contemplated the Universe and the nature of reality. These diagrams show representations of the Cosmos and, very recently, (bottom right) a modern theory of the structure of space.

In these next pages we get a sense of the majesty of the Universe we live in, from the vastness of space to the infinitesimal tininess of the atom.

There are some hidden codes on each page.
(Hint: You may need to download an app to help you.)

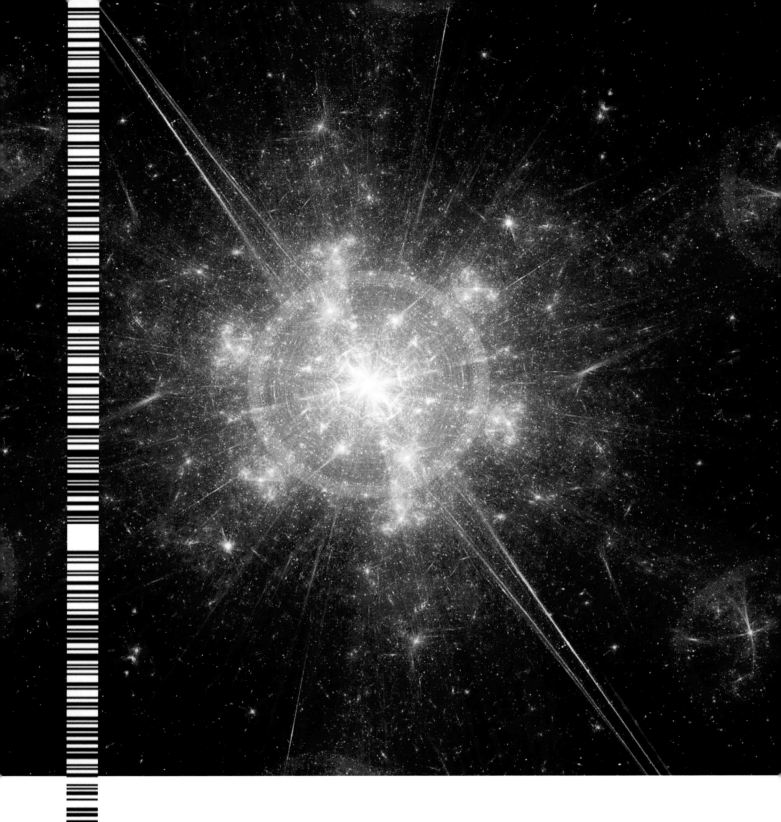

Scientists speculate that the Universe originated in a split second: The beginning of the unfolding of our known Universe.

There is an estimated 170,000,000,000 (170 billion) galaxies in the observable Universe which stretches 13.8 billion lights years from us in all directions.

We have approximately 4,000,000,000,000 (400 billion) stars in our galaxy, the Milky Way.
Some giant elliptical galaxies may have approximately 100,000,000,000,000 (100 trillion stars).

Our solar system extends 7.5 billion kilometres from the sun.
The sun releases energy at a mass-energy conversion rate of 4.26 million metric tonnes per second.

There are approximately 7,400,000,000 (7.4 Billion) Human beings on Earth today.
There are 8,700,000 (8.7 Million) estimated animal and plant species. Each species containing from one to billions of individuals.

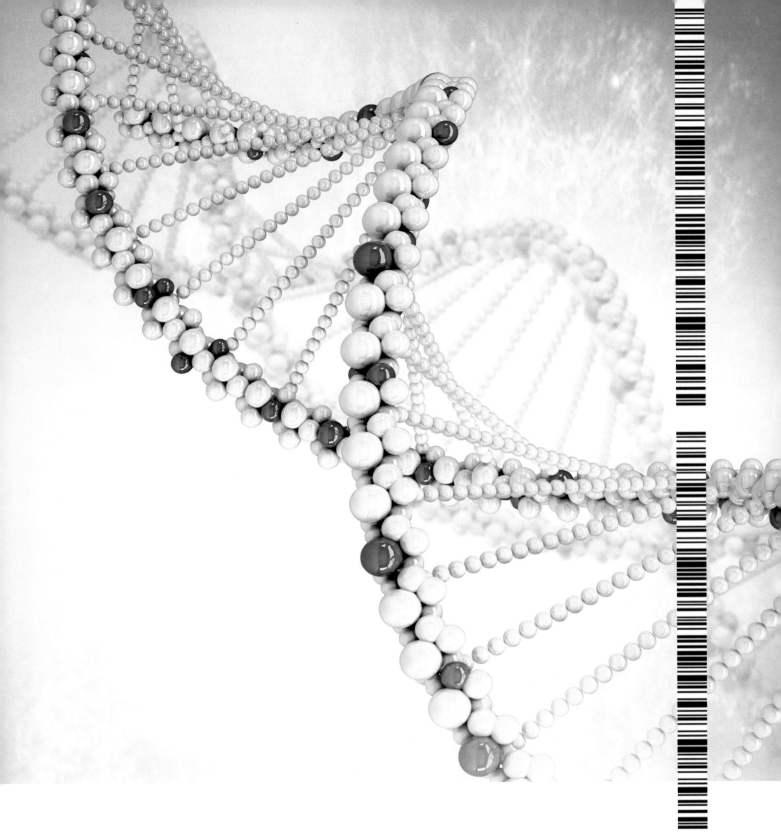

The human body has 37,200,000,000,000 (37.2 trillion) cells, each of which has tiny chemical functions that carry out the work of the cell.
Each DNA strand in each cell would stretch to 600,000,000 kilometres.

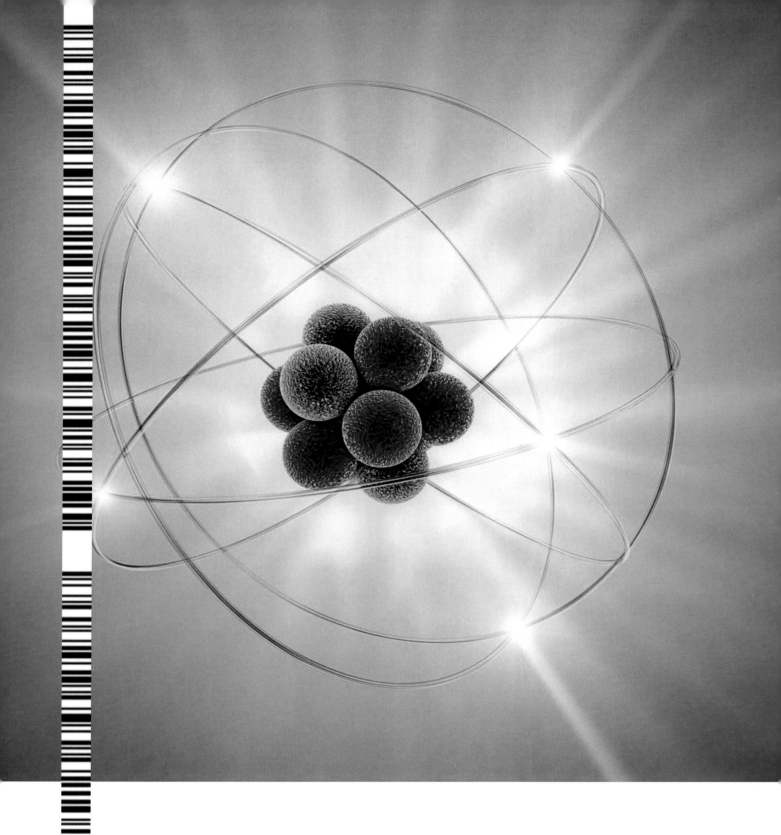

There are approximately 204,000,000,000 (204 billion) atoms in each human DNA strand. Each atom is approximately $10^{-10}m$ (0.0000000001m)

The smallest known identified particles are mainly composed of energy but shape the fabric of the Universe. Much smaller than atoms, the smallest quantum particle measures 1.6×10^{-35} m or (0.000000000000000000000000000000000016 metres) in diameter.

Acknowledgements

We thank Allah for the ability to write this book and seek His forgiveness for all flaws and inaccuracies and hope that this book will bring inspiration and happiness.

Thanks to Dr. Amira Val Baker for her in-depth knowledge, Lateefa Spiker for her wonderful illustrations, to Hana Horack-Elyafi for her beautiful calligraphy and editing skills. Thank you to Sue Conroy-Finn who also helped editing. We are also grateful to all the authors of the previous works from which we draw our sources.

Thanks also to everyone who donated money through Indigogo ® to help towards production of this book.

Notes on Islamic Sources

The book was originally inspired by Sheikh Muhammad Hisham Kabbani, a renowned scholar in Islam whose book, Approach to Armageddon, details some links with Qur'an and science. We have included a few more subjects that do not appear in Sheikh Kabbani's book. These are taken from research from other Islamic sources (see references). We have also included some Holy verses that may not have an obvious direct link with the subject matter; they are however, interesting to contemplate.

Use of the verses and translations of the Holy Qur'an

It is very difficult to translate accurately verses from Qur'an in English. This is because of the limitations of the English Language as Arabic suits the mystical nature of the Qur'an as well as its' precision and eloquence. Translation in English may slightly vary from Scholar to Scholar and we have used the translation that fits the context of the book. Allah alone knows the absolute meaning of each verse and we hope the reader will allow some flexibility in this issue.

Appendages to Holy names.

In Islam, for respect, these phrases are added after mentioning the Holy Name of Allah and of Prophet Muhammad and the other Prophets:

Allah "Jalla jalalahu" "May His Glory be Glorified."

Prophet Muhammad "Sallalahu 'alayhi wa salam" "May the blessings and the peace of Allah be upon him."
Prophets of Allah including Jesus, Moses, Noah etc "Alayhi salaam" "Upon them be peace."

References

Islamic resources

Approach to Armageddon? Sheikh Hisham Kabbani 2003
Miracles of the Quran: http://www.speed-light.info/miracles_of_quran/index.html
                              http://miraclesofthequran.com/scientific_index.html
Destiny: Reliance of the Traveller, Shafii manual of Islamic Fiqh.
Numerology in Islam: www.nurmuhammad.com
http://www.irfi.org/articles/articles_1_50/all_things_in_pair.htm
http://wafiqsyed.wordpress.com/2013/01/23/communication-of-animals-in-quran/
My Little Lore of Light by Karima Sperling 2005
The Lore of Light by Amina Adil
Quran translation: http://quran.com/100
Qur'an text: http://www.quran.gov.bd/quran/arabic/
Qur'an translation: http://corpus.quran.com/wordbyword.jsp
http://www.missionislam.com/knowledge/orignlife.html
The light of Muhammad: sunnah.org
The Qur'an Project – www.quranproject.org

i)   Hakim no. 1/555, Darimi - [Sahih]
ii)   ii)Ibn al-'Arabi Corbin, Henry. Creative Imagination in the Sufism of Ibn `Arabi, 1969. p. 185
iii)   *Allamah Ibn al-Jawzi* in his *Kitabul-Wafa* narrates a hadith from Sayyidina Abdullah ibn Abbas ☀ the cousin of the Prophet ☀ in which he said: "The Messenger of Allah had no shadow, not while standing in the sun, but the brilliance of his light (*nur*) surpassed the rays of the sun; nor while sitting before a burning light, but his luminous light excelled the lustre of the light".
iv)   Source: Ghazali, Kitab Adab Tilawat ul Qur'an

Science references

Wikipedia
Usborne Book of World Geography 1984
Usborne Encyclopedia of World History by Ted Smart
http://www.iac2012.co.za/blog/entry/the_story_of_the_two_oceans_-_where_two_worlds_meet/
http://www.physicsoftheuniverse.com/topics_relativity_emc2.html
http://www.alberteinsteinsite.com/quotes/einsteinquotes.html
Genetics: you tube, SciShow * Recommended for kids
Blown to Bits: Your Life, Liberty, and Happiness After the Digital Explosion is licensed under a Creative Commons Attribution-Noncommercial-Share Alike 3.0 United States License.
http://www.universe today.com
barcodesincl.com
http://www.askamathematician.com * good for grownups
http://www.scientificamerican.com/article/why-is-the-earths-core-so/
http://www.scientificamerican.com/article/moon-life-tides/
http://planetfacts.org/why-is-the-moon-important/
Sir Issac newton: BBC documentary, Newton the Dark Heretic
http://neptune.atlantis-intl.com/dolphins/sounds.html
Quotes by Max Plank: www.resonance.is *"As a man who has devoted his whole life to the most clear headed science, to the study of matter, I can tell you as a result of my research about atoms this much: There is no matter as such. All matter originates and exists only by virtue of a force which brings the particle of an atom to vibration and holds this most minute solar system of the atom together. We must assume behind this force the existence of a conscious and intelligent mind. This mind is the matrix of all matter."*
Nassim Harramein: http://www.resonance.is
Biocentrism by Robert Lanza 2010

Images

Image credits: Most images and photographs are from Dreamstime.com. image bank, various artists and photographers (please contact author for specifics) except:
Space images from Nasa, general copyright. http://www.nasa.gov/multimedia/guidelines/index.html
Mountain Roots image – Yasmin Watson
Orbital patterns – Howard Arrington Dances of the Planets 2013
Prophet Muhammads (uhbp) hair – Shazaib Hussain
Image King Soloman and the hoopoe bird courtesy of the Harvard Art Museum.
Plate boundaries: by passmyexams.com
By NASA Earth Observatory images by Robert Simmon and Jesse Allen, using Landsat data from the USGS Earth Explorer. Caption by Adam Voiland. - Faults in Xinjiang (Nasa Earth Observatory), Public Domain,.
Astronomy:Istanbul University library. https://www.flickr.com/photos/47254367@N02/4332348124/in/photostream/ by Marie-Pierre Langen general license to reuse : https://creativecommons.org/licenses/by-sa/2.0/

Key to hidden codes: Barcodes have been places in each image. Download an app on your phone to read barcodes, scan the whitest barcode to reveal the answer...

Heavenly Homework

Some verses in the Holy Qur'an challenged writers who were sceptical to produce a book like it:

"And if ye are in doubt as to what We have revealed from time to time to Our Servant, then produce a Sura like thereunto; and call your witnesses or helpers (If there are any) besides God, if your (doubts) are true." (Baqara:23)

Imagine then, if your homework assignment was to write a religious book that includes religious and moral guidance, lessons from the lives of the peoples of the past, the messages of the Prophets, the physical sciences and historical accounts of important events.

Approximately 80,000 words

Try to include the following;

1. Use rhymed prose using your language but a more special version, one that has not been heard before, yet entirely convincing.

2. Ensure that at least 80% of the rhymes use only three sounds from your alphabet and at the same time be eloquent, beautiful and informative.

3. Make it is easy to memorise.

4. Prepare your book around at least one number so that this number forms the underlying structure of your text.

5. Imbed some outstanding number coincidences about interesting things about our world or Universe.

6. Include subtle references to facts about chemical elements in the Universe.

7. Include statements revealing some secrets of life

8. Ensure that people will still be interested in it 1500 years in the future.

9. Have many layers of meaning, from every day concerns to elevated moral and spiritual concepts.

10. Be entirely original and not sound like other religious books.

Printed in the USA
CPSIA information can be obtained
at www.ICGtesting.com
LVRC082326210224
772322LV00008B/82